Andrew Cousins is a Barrister at DWF Advocacy Limited and advises on a wide range of civil litigation matters. Andrew qualified as a Legal Executive in 2006, a Solicitor in 2011 and was called to the Bar by the Honourable Society of the Middle Temple in 2017. Andrew has a background in personal injury, coronial and regulatory law. Andrew has advised clients in respect of CRU issues from the outset of a claim up to and including appearing before the Social Entitlement Chamber on behalf of Compensators in CRU appeals. Andrew has advised both Claimants and Defendants in relation to personal injury and CRU work and has given a number of training presentations on this area of law.

A Practical Guide to the Compensation Recovery Unit and NHS Charges in Personal Injury Claims in England & Wales

A Practical Guide to the Compensation Recovery Unit and NHS Charges in Personal Injury Claims in England & Wales

Andrew Cousins
Barrister, Middle Temple
LLM MRes

Law Brief Publishing

Published 2020 by Law Brief Publishing, an imprint of Law Brief Publishing Ltd
30 The Parks
Minehead
Somerset
TA24 8BT

www.lawbriefpublishing.com

Paperback: 978-1-912687-82-4

To my skydiving family.

For all your support.

PREFACE

When I began writing this practical guide, my intention was to provide a concise handbook to assist practitioners in addressing the main issues facing them when considering Compensation Recovery Unit ('CRU') situations in a personal injury or disease claim. Issues regarding the CRU need to be considered at numerous stages of a claim, including post settlement, yet they are sometimes forgotten or sidelined whilst the substantive claim is dealt with.

This is an area of law that can often cause difficulties, and it is layered with complexities in terms of legislation, statutory instruments and tribunal procedures. Personal injury practitioners will be aware that the calculations involved in offsetting damages are just one aspect of the work involved with the CRU. Calculating how to offset benefits from settlement offers, and determining whether a judgment is more or less advantageous than a relevant settlement offer can cause complications both for practitioners, and for a judge presiding over a trial. Additionally the process for a Compensator or Injured Person in reviewing and/or appealing a Certificate of Recoverable Benefits can be a lengthy process, which requires an analytical approach to the evidence, this can prove to be time consuming and costly. These are just some of the issues that frequently arise in this field of law.

Throughout the course of this book, I have tried to focus on the practical aspects of this area of law, so that the book can be as useful as possible to those who have to grapple with these issues in practise. Whilst I have addressed the background to the CRU in the first chapter, I have tried to steer away from a historical review of how the CRU came to exist, in order to focus on day to day practical issues.

I do not by any means claim to be the preeminent expert in the field of CRU work, there are many lawyers and academics with a detailed knowledge of the law and the issues in this area which will easily surpass my own. The matters set out in this book address issues that frequently occur in dealing with the CRU, and the framework around this area of law.

This book is not meant to be a comprehensive analysis of benefits law, how benefits are awarded and calculated. Whilst I have set out in chapter two some information about the types of benefits applicable to the CRU, it is not my intention to engage in a lengthy analysis of the legal framework and tests behind each type of benefit. The book aims to address how the CRU interacts with compensation claims and how practitioners may approach the various situations that can arise as cases progress.

This book is directed towards practitioners of all levels who operate in the field of personal injury work, but will be most helpful for practitioners who are new to the field and have not had the opportunity to gather much experience in this area of law.

It is not my intention in this book to address how the CRU interacts with clinical negligence claims. I have not addressed clinical negligence claims as the CRU has a team of specialists who deal with such cases. In these claims, consideration must be given to the multitude of causation issues that need to be considered, in order to determine what benefits, and how much of them, were paid as a result of the alleged clinical negligence, because of its bespoke nature it is not proposed to address this area of work in this book. Likewise, I have not addressed the issue of foreign compensators, as the law in this regard is, to an extent, dependent upon the law applicable to which country the Compensator is based. This is not an issue that arises frequently, and this book is designed to address issues that frequently arise in the jurisdiction of England and Wales. The law as set out and quoted in this book is believed to be accurate as of 15 June 2020.

In closing, I would like to pass on my thanks to Tim Kevan and Garry Wright at Law Brief Publishing Ltd for all of their support throughout this project, and to David Boyle of Deans Court Chambers. David is a

Barrister and respected author of a number of books, and his guidance throughout my first attempt at authorship has been thoroughly appreciated and much needed!

Andrew Cousins
June 2020

GLOSSARY

Appeal	The process by which a Compensator or Injured Person may challenge the decision of the CRU in relation to recoupment of applicable benefits and/or NHS charges.
Calderbank offer	A settlement offer made by a party in the substantive litigation.
Certificate of recoverable benefits	The certificate issued by the CRU, which informs the Compensator which recoverable benefits, and lump sum payments have been paid, or will likely be paid. Also provides the Compensator the figure for the total amount of benefits to be repaid to the Secretary of State.
Certificate of NHS charges	The certificate issued by the CRU, which informs the Compensator what NHS treatment was provided to the Injured Person. In addition, details the number of days of treatment provided, whether there are any ambulance charges and the total amount of NHS charges to be repaid to the Secretary of State.
Compensation payment	A payment made by way of compensation for an accident, injury or a disease. A payment which can be made in varying forms of monetary or non-monetary manners.

Compensation recovery unit	A branch of the Department for Work and Pensions that works directly with insurance companies and solicitors to recover applicable benefits paid by the state, as a result of injury or disease, when a compensation payment has been made.
Compensator	The person or entity who caused the injury or disease sustained by the Injured Person.
Contributory negligence	A partial defence available to a Compensator under the Law Reform (Contributory Negligence) Act (1945), where it is proved that the Injured Person's own negligence contributed to the loss. Provides for an apportionment of loss where the fault of both the Injured Person and the Compensator/s contributed to the loss.
CRU1	Form completed by the Compensator at the outset of the case to register the matter with the CRU.
CRU102	Form completed by the Compensator at the conclusion of the case to notify the CRU of the outcome of the claim.
CRU250	Form issued by the CRU if the CRU has not been notified of the outcome of the claim two years post registration.
Exempt payment	A payment specifically exempt from the provisions of the Social Security (Recovery of Benefits) Act (1997), the

	Social Security (Recovery of Benefits) (Lump Sum Payments) Regulations (2008) and the Social Security (Recovery of Benefits) (Lump Sum Payments) (Amendment) Regulations (2014).
Ex gratia payment	A payment made by a Compensator without an imposition of liability upon them to do so.
Injured person	The person claiming compensation following the suffering of alleged loss and damage.
Interim payment	A payment made by the Compensator to the Injured Person for an amount of money paid, before the total sum of damages is either agreed or awarded.
Joint settlement meeting	A meeting attended by some or all of the parties to the substantive litigation, with a view to reaching settlement of some or all aspects of the claim.
Mandatory reconsideration	The process by which a Compensator or Injured Person may formally seek a reconsideration of the Certificate of Recoverable Benefits, prior to any appeal being made.
Multiple compensator case	A case where there is one incident, but more than one Compensator is involved.
Offeree	Party to the substantive litigation receiving an offer of settlement.

Offeror	Party to the substantive litigation making an offer of settlement.
Offsetting of recoverable benefits	The process by which recoverable benefits listed on the Certificate of Recoverable Benefits are deducted from the settlement offer, agreed settlement sum or award of damages.
Part 36 offer	An offer of settlement, which complies with Part 36 of the Civil Procedure Rules.
Recoverable benefits	The applicable benefits listed in Schedule 2 of the Social Security (Recovery of Benefits) Act (1997), and paid in the Relevant Period.
Recoverable lump sums	Payments made under the Pneumoconiosis etc. (Workers' Compensation) Act (1979), the 2008 Diffuse Mesothelioma Scheme, the 2014 Diffuse Mesothelioma Payment Scheme (DMPS) or an ex-statutory payment that was paid because the person did not qualify for a payment under the aforesaid 1979 Workers' Compensation Act.
Relevant period	The period of time in respect of which applicable social security benefits and NHS charges may be recovered.
Review	The process by which a Compensator or Injured Person may ask the CRU to reconsider any aspect of the Certificate of Recoverable Benefits.

Settlement date	The date on which the compensation payment is made to the Injured Person.
Structured settlements	A settlement agreement entered into between the Compensator and the Injured Person, for the making of lump sum payments and periodical payments.

LEGISLATION, STATUTORY INSTRUMENTS AND CASE LAW`

Legislation

- Child Maintenance and Other Payments Act (2008)
- Fatal Accidents Act (1976)
- Health and Social Care (Community Health and Standards) Act (2003)
- Law Reform (Miscellaneous Provisions) Act (1934)
- Limitation Act (1980)
- Pneumoconiosis etc. (Workers' Compensation) Act 1979
- Social Security Administration Act (1992)
- Social Security (Recovery of Benefits Act) (1997)
- The Mesothelioma Act (2014)
- The Social Security Act (1998)
- Welfare Reform Act (2012)

Statutory Instruments

- The Personal Injuries (NHS Charges) (General) and Road Traffic (NHS Charges) (Amendment) Regulations (2006)
- The Social Security (Recovery of Benefits) Regulations (1997)
- The Social Security (Recovery of Benefits) (Lump Sum Payments) Regulations (2008)

- The Social Security (Recovery of Benefits) (Lump Sum Payments) (Amendment) Regulations (2014)

Case Law

- Calderbank v Calderbank [1975] 3 All ER 333 (EWCA)
- Clenshaw v Tanner [2002] EWCA Civ 1848
- Colin Crooks v Hendricks Lovell Limited [2016] EWCA Civ 8
- Davies v Inman [1999] P.I.Q.R. Q26
- Denton v TH White Ltd [2014] EWCA Civ 906
- Griffiths and others v British Coal Corporation and another [2001] EWCA Civ 336
- Hassall & Pether v Secretary of State for Social Security [1995] 3 All ER 909
- Helen Williams v Devon County Council [2003] EWCA Civ 365
- Hilton International Hotels v Smith [1002] PIQR P14
- Hodgson v Trapp [1989] A.C. 807
- Kadir v Mistry & Ors [2014] EWCA Civ 1177
- McCaffery v Datta (Costs) [1997] 1 W.L.R. 870
- Mitchell v Laing [1998] The Times, January 28
- Momonakaya v the Ministry of Defence [2019] EWHC 480 (QB)

- Mr Trevor Fox v Foundation Piling Limited [2011] EWCA Civ 790
- Parry v Cleaver [1970] A.C. 1
- Re: British Coal Respiratory Disease Litigation [2000] All ER (D) 1552
- Rees v West Glamorgan County Council [1994] P.I.Q.R. P37
- Wisely v John Fulton (Plumbers) Ltd and the linked appeal of Wadey v Surrey County Council [2000] 1 WLR 820
- Williams v Devon CC [2003] EWCA Civ 365

CONTENTS

CHAPTER ONE
BACKGROUND TO THE COMPENSATION RECOVERY UNIT

In ***Parry v Cleaver [1970] A.C. 1***, Lord Reid identified two salient questions about how a Plaintiff (now Claimant) should be compensated:

> *"First, what did the plaintiff lose as a result of the accident? What are the sums which he would have received but for the accident but which by reason of the accident he can no longer get? And, secondly, what are the sums which he did in fact receive as a result of the accident but which he would not have received if there had been no accident? And then the question arises whether the latter sums must be deducted from the former in assessing the damages."*

In England and Wales, an Injured Person may well be in receipt of state benefits after being involved in an accident or developing a disease. The question that arises is how those benefits should be taken into account, if at all, when damages come to be assessed. Lord Reid's judgment is often cited as the foundation principle that the state paid benefit monies must be deducted from the Injured Person's damages when assessing compensation, in order to prevent the Injured Person being over-compensated.

Since 6 October 1997, all compensation payments made as a result of an accident, injury or disease, and paid on behalf of a person compensating an Injured Person in respect of that accident, injury or disease, are subject to deductions of applicable state benefits. The current scheme came into existence on that date, and whilst there were rules in place before 1997, there is little point in discussing those in detail as they are no longer of any real use to practitioners. Those who practised in the field of personal injury claims prior to the introduction of the Social Security (Recovery of Benefits) Act (1997) will recall that the offsetting of benefits was treated very differently. For a time, the state recouped benefits payments from any head of loss claimed, including damages for pain, suffering and loss of amenity, once the damages awarded exceeded £2,500. This position was considered unfair, as damages awarded for pain suffering and loss of amenity were not associated with the payment of state benefits, and Injured Persons were unfairly deprived of a portion of their compensation.

The rationale behind the current recovery of benefits scheme is that it operates as a clawback by the Department for Work and Pensions. It allows the government to recover benefit monies from a Compensator who has admitted causing, or been found by a civil court to have caused, injury, disease or loss to a Claimant and who is paying compensation which reflects, or touches upon, the types of benefit which have been received. The introduction of the Social Security (Recovery of Benefits) Act (1997) changed the legislative landscape, in that there is no longer any right to recoup benefit payments from damages for pain, suffering and loss of amenity. Such damages are now 'ring fenced' and cannot be affected by payments of state benefits, although there are some exceptions that are discussed in chapter five.

The current rules require a like for like deduction from damages of the amounts of certain listed state benefits paid to the Injured Person by the Department for Work and Pensions between the date of injury and the resolution of the claim, with a cap of five years from the date of injury. The scheme derives from the general rule set out by the House of Lords in ***Hodgson v Trapp [1989] A.C. 807***, that a Claimant must give credit for benefits which have accrued as a result of an accident which is the substance of the litigation.

The key pieces of legislation enacted in relation to the Compensation Recovery Unit ('CRU') are the ***Social Security (Recovery of Benefits)***

Act (1997), ('Recovery of Benefits Act'), the ***Health and Social Care (Community Health and Standards) Act (2003)***, ('Health and Social Care Act'), and the ***Welfare Reform Act (2012)***, ('Welfare Reform Act'). Whilst there is a significant amount of legislation and statutory instruments in this field, these Acts underpin this area of law.

The Recovery of Benefits Act established the current legislative framework for imposing liabilities on Compensators to repay state benefits, and also set out the ways by which benefits could be offset against heads of damage claimed by the Injured Person. The Health and Social Care Act established the framework for the recovery of NHS charges, and the Welfare Reform Act made amendments to the types of applicable benefits which could be offset and paid.

Imposition of liability

Since the enactment of the Recovery of Benefits Act, a person who makes a payment in respect of an accident, injury or disease suffered by another, has been required to repay recoverable benefits to the Secretary of State. As set out in ***Goff & Jones The Law of Unjust Enrichment 9th Ed. 19-44*** the legislation:

> *effectively give the NHS and the (renamed) Department for Work and Pensions a right to reimbursement from tortfeasors who would otherwise be unjustly enriched at their expense if the damages that they were liable to pay were reduced by the amount of benefit or care received by their victims.*

The right of the Secretary of State to recover the benefits from the Compensator is set out at ***s6(1) Recovery of Benefits Act:***

> *A person who makes a compensation payment in any case is liable to pay to the Secretary of State an amount equal to the total amount of the recoverable benefits.*

This statutory provision imposes a liability on the Compensator to repay to the Secretary of State, benefits listed on the Certificate of Recoverable Benefits ('CRB'). The CRU administers the scheme for the recovery of these monies on behalf of the Secretary of State. The CRU works with insurance companies, solicitors and Injured Persons, to recover social security benefits and NHS charges. The issue of NHS charges will be addressed in a separate chapter later in this book.

The CRU's website (https://www.gov.uk/government/collections/cru), sets out that it has two stated aims, these are:

- *to recover amounts of social security benefits paid as a result of an accident, injury or disease, if a compensation payment has been made; and*

- *to recover costs incurred by NHS hospitals and Ambulance Trusts for treatment from injuries from road traffic accidents and personal injury claims.*

Accrual and cessation of liability

The liability on the Compensator can arise at different times depending upon the type of case that is being brought against the Compensator. The date from which the CRU can recover benefits from is:

1. the day following an accident or injury or

2. in disease cases the date that an applicable benefit is first claimed as a result of the disease

As can be seen in, for example, a case concerning a road traffic accident, the date from which benefits can start to accrue is often very clear and causes little difficulty. In cases concerning for example, injuries attributable to asbestos where there may be no definitive date of exposure, the date can be less clearly assigned as it is not always certain when the medical condition first developed. A Compensator may be well advised to carefully examine the CRB upon receipt and consider whether the benefits listed have been paid as a consequence of the injury or disease, or because of other causes not associated with the substantive claim brought against the Compensator.

A Compensator is not liable to repay benefits paid otherwise than in relation to the accident, injury or disease, and may wish to challenge any benefits listed on the CRB that are not linked to the substantive claim. The Review and Appeals process, by which a Compensator takes such action, is covered in a later chapter in this book.

The date on which the Compensator's liability for state benefits ceases is:

1. the day a compensation payment is made in final discharge of a claim or

2. the date an agreement is made between the Compensator and injured person under which an earlier compensation payment is treated as having been made in final discharge of any claim or

3. the date five years after the relevant recovery period begins, whichever comes first

As readers will note, point three above outlines the term 'relevant recovery period', this is a term defined in ***s3 Recovery of Benefits Act*** which provides:

> *(1) In relation to a person ("the claimant") who has suffered any accident, injury or disease, "the relevant period" has the meaning given by the following subsections.*

(2) Subject to subsection (4), if it is a case of accident or injury, the relevant period is the period of five years immediately following the day on which the accident or injury in question occurred.

(3) Subject to subsection (4), if it is a case of disease, the relevant period is the period of five years beginning with the date on which the claimant first claims a listed benefit in consequence of the disease.

(4) If at any time before the end of the period referred to in sub-section (2) or (3)—

(a) a person makes a compensation payment in final discharge of any claim made by or in respect of the claimant and arising out of the accident, injury or disease, or

(b) an agreement is made under which an earlier compensation payment is treated as having been made in final discharge of any such claim, the relevant period ends at that time.

The date on which a Compensator ceases to be liable for state benefits does not cause a difficulty in the majority of cases. The claim for damages is settled at the stage the Compensator repays the benefits, the claim does not succeed (in which case of course no liability to repay the benefits falls on the Compensator), or the five-year point is reached. At any of these points, the Compensator's liability to repay the applicable benefits ceases.

The position is more complicated though if an appeal in the substantive claim is launched after a trial. In such a situation, the parties should take note of the position expounded by Professor Lewis in his book *Deducting Benefits from Damages for Personal Injury Claims*. At *s13.14,* it is noted that, pursuant to the rule in ***Mitchell v Laing (1998) The Times, January 28***, where a case is concluded by way of a Court order and not by way of a settlement, the 'cutoff date' is not the date of the Court order, but the date of the payment of the sum awarded. This means that if the judgment is appealed, the recovery period of applicable benefits can continue until the payment of any damages awarded. Therefore, during the life of the appeal, benefits may still accrue, and thus the Compensator's liability increases.

Non-personal injury claims

This book is aimed at addressing personal injury claims, so I will not dwell on the recovery of benefits in non-personal injury claims, but there are two instances that are worth noting. The CRU's website contains a very helpful Technical Note. This Technical Note is referred to in a number of sections in this book, it can be found at https://www.gov.uk/government/publications/recovery-of-benefits-and-or-lump-sum-payments-and-nhs-charges-technical-guidance/recovery-of-benefits-and-lump-sum-payments-and-nhs-charges-technical-guidance. This Technical Note also addresses the applicability of the scheme in relation to property damage claims, professional negligence claims and goodwill payments. Even though they are not claims arising from personal injury or disease matters, in certain circumstances the scheme can apply to such claims. In relation to property damage claims, the CRU Technical Note asserts:

> *You must notify CRU on form CRU1 if a claim for property damage includes:*
>
> - *a claim for loss of earnings*
> - *a loss of mobility*
> - *cost of care*
> - *any other element of compensation*

In relation to professional negligence claims, the CRU Technical Note asserts:

> *Where a claim is made for professional negligence and the particulars of claim, statement of claim or letter before action includes a claim for compensation as a result of the original accident, injury or disease, form CRU1 must be submitted and any listed benefits and lump sum payment paid in consequence of the original accident, injury or disease will be recoverable.*

Finally, in relation to goodwill payments, the CRU Technical Note asserts:

> *A goodwill payment, usually in the form of gift vouchers or the like, is sometimes made in response to a complaint about a product or incident. For example, if someone slips in a retailer's premises and only suffers a minor injury, inconvenience or embarrassment or if the consumption of foodstuffs is alleged to have caused a stomach complaint.*
>
> *If such a payment is made at the time of the complaint or incident, CRU does not need to be informed.*
>
> *However, if such a payment is made at a later date, benefits or NHS treatment may have been received. In these cases, a form CRU1 must be submitted, especially compensation is being sought in respect of:*
>
> - *loss of earnings*
> - *cost of care*
> - *loss of mobility*

As such, a Compensator can be liable to repay applicable benefits in certain non-personal injury claims, where the nature of the claim includes a claim for damages where the Claimant may already have received state benefits. These situations can arise where litigants in person advance their own claims but seek to, for example, only claim for lost earnings caused by the Compensator's negligence. The Compensator has to be alive to the fact that such a payment may render them liable to also repay any applicable benefits.

Exempt Payments

Whilst the above legislation imposes a liability on Compensators to repay recoverable benefits to the Secretary of State, there are certain situations where the Compensator does not have to repay the recoverable benefits. ***Schedule 1 Recovery of Benefits Act*** makes provision for certain compensation payments to be classified as 'exempt payments' and thus a liability to repay benefits to the Secretary of State does not arise. ***Schedule 1*** provides that recovery will not be made from the following types of payments:

1. *Any small payment (defined in Part II of this Schedule).*

2. *Any payment made to or for the injured person under section 130 of the Powers of Criminal Courts (Sentencing) Act] 2000, section 8 of the Modern Slavery Act 2015, section 175 of the Armed Forces Act 2006 or section 249 of the Criminal Procedure (Scotland) Act 1995 (compensation orders against convicted persons).*

3. *Any payment made in the exercise of a discretion out of property held subject to a trust in a case where no more than 50 per cent. by value of the capital contributed to the trust was directly or indirectly provided by persons who are, or are alleged to be, liable in respect of —*

(a) the accident, injury or disease suffered by the injured person, or

(b) the same or any connected accident, injury or disease suffered by another.

4. *Any payment made out of property held for the purposes of any prescribed trust (whether the payment also falls within paragraph 3 or not).*

5. *(1) Any payment made to the injured person by an insurer] under the terms of any contract of insurance entered into between the injured person and the insurer] before—*

(a) the date on which the injured person first claims a listed benefit in consequence of the disease in question, or

(b) the occurrence of the accident or injury in question.

(2)"Insurer" means—

(a) a person who has permission under Part 4, Part 4A of the Financial Services and Markets Act 2000 to effect or carry out contracts of insurance; or

(b) an EEA firm of the kind mentioned in paragraph 5(d) of Schedule 3 to that Act which has permission under paragraph 15 of that Schedule (as a result of qualifying for authorisation under paragraph 12 of that Schedule) to effect or carry out contracts of insurance.

(3)Sub-paragraph (2) must be read with—

(a) section 22 of the Financial Services and Markets Act 2000;

(b) any relevant order under that section; and

(c) Schedule 2 to that Act.

6. *Any redundancy payment falling to be taken into account in the assessment of damages in respect of an accident, injury or disease.*

7. *So much of any payment as is referable to costs.*

8. *Any prescribed payment.*

Many of these sections require secondary legislation to be brought forwards before they are implemented. As a consequence they are rarely seen in practice, and Compensators are best reminded that they have a statutory obligation to repay applicable benefits unless otherwise relieved of that obligation.

CHAPTER TWO
TYPES OF APPLICABLE BENEFITS

As set out in the introduction to this book, this work is not intended to be an in-depth analysis of benefits law and how benefits are awarded and calculated. This chapter is designed to give a brief explanation as to the types of benefits that are applicable under the ***Recovery of Benefits Act***.

Not all benefit payments are required to be considered when addressing CRU issues in personal injury claims. The relevant benefits are set out in ***Schedule 2 Recovery of Benefits Act***. This Schedule lists the benefits which need to be considered when calculating the compensation payment being made to the Injured Person. The information below is designed to provide the reader with some background to the specifics of individual applicable benefits, more detailed information relating to these benefits can be seen at https://www.gov.uk/browse/benefits. The relevant benefits are:

1. Universal Credit
2. Disablement pension payable under s103 of the Social Security Contributions and Benefits Act (1992)
3. Employment and support allowance
4. Incapacity benefit
5. Income support
6. Invalidity pension and allowance
7. Jobseeker's allowance
8. Reduced earnings allowance

9. Severe disablement allowance
10. Sickness benefit
11. Unemployability supplement
12. Unemployment benefit
13. Attendance allowance
14. Daily living component of personal independence payment
15. Care component of disability living allowance
16. Disablement pension increase payable under section 104 or 105 of the Social Security Contributions and Benefits Act (1992)
17. Mobility allowance
18. Mobility component of personal independence payment
19. Mobility component of disability living allowance

Not all of these benefits will appear on every CRB, and some benefits are listed more frequently than others. Indeed, it is quite rare to see some of the benefits that are listed below, particularly some of the unemployment and pension benefits.

Universal credit

Universal Credit ('UC') was introduced by ***s1 Welfare Reform Act (2012)***. It replaced a number of benefit payments which were abolished by ***s33 Welfare Reform Act (2012)***, these were:

(a) income-based jobseeker's allowance under the Jobseekers Act 1995;

(b) income-related employment and support allowance under Part 1 of the Welfare Reform Act 2007;

(c) income support under section 124 of the Social Security Contributions and Benefits Act 1992;

(d) housing benefit under section 130 of that Act;

(e) council tax benefit under section 131 of that Act;

(f) child tax credit and working tax credit under the Tax Credits Act 2002.

UC is a benefit designed to help with living costs and is calculated by reference to a number of provisions, ***s1(3) Welfare Reform Act (2012)***, sets these out:

(a) a standard allowance,

(b) an amount for responsibility for children or young persons,

(c) an amount for housing, and

(d) amounts for other particular needs or circumstances.

As can be seen, UC is an 'umbrella benefit' that encompasses several different types of payments. It remains open to be seen whether a challenge may be brought to determine whether all of the payments in ***s1(3)*** of the Act can be attributable to the Injured Person's accident or disease. Thus far, no case has reached the Upper Tier Tribunal to determine this issue.

Disablement pension payable under s103 of the Social Security Contributions and Benefits Act (1992)

If this benefit is registered on a CRB, it is important to consider the Injured Person's assessment of disability at the medical examination, as the award of the benefit is contingent upon the Injured Person being restricted, physically or mentally, to a recognised percentage level.

s103 Social Security Contributions and Benefits Act (1992), provides:

> *(1) Subject to the provisions of this section, an employed earner shall be entitled to disablement pension if he suffers as the result of the relevant accident from loss of physical or mental faculty such that the assessed extent of the resulting disablement amounts to not less than 14 per cent. or, on a claim made before 1st October 1986, 20 per cent.*

Employment and support allowance

An Injured Person can be eligible for Employment and Support Allowance (ESA), if they have a disability or health condition that affects how much they can work. Much like the awarding of UC, the purpose of the ESA benefit is to give the Injured Person assistance with living costs during the time when they are unable to work.

The benefit has a secondary purpose of providing residual support to the Injured Person during their return to work when they may still be suffering some restrictions on working abilities. In order to qualify for ESA, the Injured Person must be below the state pension age and have a disability or health condition that affects their ability to work. An Injured Person is not eligible for ESA if:

a) The Injured Person is in receipt of severe disability premium, or is entitled to its receipt;

b) The Injured Person is in receipt of Statutory Sick Pay (SSP) from an employer.

Incapacity benefit

Incapacity Benefit is being replaced with Employment and Support Allowance (ESA), it will therefore appear on fewer CRB's as time progresses. The DWP are currently reviewing Injured Persons in receipt of Incapacity Benefit to determine if they are entitled to claim ESA. Any benefits paid for Incapacity Benefit will therefore be historic. This benefit was designed to be paid to Injured Persons who faced difficulties in returning to work owing to long-term illness or disability.

Income support

Income Support is designed to assist persons on a low income, the Injured Person does not have to be completely unable to work in order to receive Income Support, if the Injured Person does not work many hours, Income Support can be used to 'top up' their income.

Income support is a 'means tested benefit', therefore any entitlement to the benefit is based on the Injured Person's income, savings and other capital, which will be considered when the DWP decide if the Injured Person qualifies for the benefit. As set out under the UC section above, Income Support is being replaced by UC. Like Incapacity Benefit, it will therefore feature on fewer certificates moving forward.

Invalidity pension and allowance

Invalidity Pension is a benefit paid on a weekly basis to an Injured Person people who cannot work because of a long-term illness or disability. In order to receive this benefit, the Injured Person must have

b) The Injured Person is in receipt of Statutory Sick Pay (SSP) from an employer.

Incapacity benefit

Incapacity Benefit is being replaced with Employment and Support Allowance (ESA), it will therefore appear on fewer CRB's as time progresses. The DWP are currently reviewing Injured Persons in receipt of Incapacity Benefit to determine if they are entitled to claim ESA. Any benefits paid for Incapacity Benefit will therefore be historic. This benefit was designed to be paid to Injured Persons who faced difficulties in returning to work owing to long-term illness or disability.

Income support

Income Support is designed to assist persons on a low income, the Injured Person does not have to be completely unable to work in order to receive Income Support, if the Injured Person does not work many hours, Income Support can be used to 'top up' their income.

Income support is a 'means tested benefit', therefore any entitlement to the benefit is based on the Injured Person's income, savings and other capital, which will be considered when the DWP decide if the Injured Person qualifies for the benefit. As set out under the UC section above, Income Support is being replaced by UC. Like Incapacity Benefit, it will therefore feature on fewer certificates moving forward.

Invalidity pension and allowance

Invalidity Pension is a benefit paid on a weekly basis to an Injured Person who cannot work because of a long-term illness or disability. In order to receive this benefit, the Injured Person must have been incapable of work for at least 12 months and be likely to be incapable of work for at least another 12 months.

In the alternative, the Injured Person may be permanently incapable of work and qualify for this benefit. As can be seen, the nature of the medical assessment will be crucial to the award or refusal of this benefit.

Jobseeker's allowance

An Injured Person can apply for Jobseeker's Allowance ('JSA') to provide them with assistance whilst they are actively looking for work. There are three different types of JSA:

- 'New style' JSA
- Contribution based JSA
- Income based JSA

To qualify for 'new style' JSA the Injured Person will need to demonstrate that they are actively seeking employment and that they have worked as an employee and have paid Class 1 National Insurance contributions, or National Insurance Credits within the last two to three years.

To qualify for contribution based JSA, the Injured Person will need to demonstrate that they are actively seeking employment and that they have worked as an employee and paid Class 1 National Insurance contributions, or National Insurance Credits within the last two to three years. Unlike the 'new style' JSA the Injured Person can be performing a degree of work and still be eligible for the benefit, as long as they are working less than 16 hours per week on average.

Severe disablement allowance

Severe Disablement Allowance ('SDA') has been replaced with ESA, as such there will be a diminishing number of certificates which list this as a benefit. A re-assessment is currently taking place to determine if Injured Persons currently in receipt of SDA are eligible for ESA.

Sickness benefit

This benefit is a simple benefit designed to assist Injured Persons who have been absent from work due to ill health or injury. In practise other applicable benefits often appear on the CRB in place of this benefit.

Unemployability supplement

Unemployability Supplement ('US') is another benefit that is becoming historic. It was paid to Injured Persons who suffered industrial injuries, but no new claims have been accepted since 6 April 1987, when Industrial Injuries Disablement Benefit was increased. Injured Persons in receipt of US as at 6 April 1987 have been allowed to continue to receive the benefit if they satisfy the benefit criteria.

Unemployment benefit

The benefit is designed to assist those with employment difficulties, in practise other applicable benefits often appear on the CRB in place of this benefit.

Attendance allowance

Attendance Allowance ('AA') is designed to assist with payment of the extra costs of having someone look after a disabled Injured Person. In order to qualify for AA the Injured Person must be of state pension age and have a disability that requires someone else to provide care and assistance for the Injured Person.

An Injured Person cannot receive AA if they already receive Disability Living Allowance or Personal Independence Payment.

Daily living component of personal independence payment

Daily Living Component of Personal Independence Payment is designed to help an Injured Person with some of the extra living costs of their long-term health condition or disability.

In order to qualify for this benefit the Injured Person must be aged 16 or over and have not reached the state pension age. The Injured Person must also have a disability that affects the Injured Person to the extent that they have difficulties with daily living for a three-month period. These difficulties must be expected to continue for at least nine months.

Care component of disability living allowance

The care component of disability living allowance is designed to assist Injured Persons who have care needs as a result of an illness or disability that affect their daily life, the benefit is not means tested.

There are three rates of payment, the lower rate, the middle rate and the higher rate. The rates are graded according to the level of care required by the Injured Person, and ranges from simple assistance with cooking meals for example (the lowest rate), up to and including provisions for assistance frequently throughout the day and night (the highest rate).

Disablement Pension Increase Payable under section 104 or 105 of the Social Security Contributions and Benefits Act (1992)

If the Injured Person is in receipt of a disablement pension but suffers a loss of faculty rendering them in need of constant attendance, the disablement pension can be increased. If the Injured Person is receiving medical treatment as an in-patient at a hospital, then the level of the increase in the pension may be subject to a further increased revision.

The provisions of the Act state:

(1) Where a disablement pension is payable in respect of an assessment of 100 per cent., then, if as the result of the relevant loss of faculty the beneficiary requires constant attendance, the weekly rate of the pension shall be increased by an amount, not exceeding the appropriate amount specified in Schedule 4, Part V, paragraph 2 determined in accordance with regulations by reference to the extent and nature of the attendance required by the beneficiary.

S105

(1) Where a disablement pension is payable to a person—

(a) who is or, but for having received medical or other treatment as an in-patient in a hospital or similar institution, would be entitled to an increase of the weekly rate of the pension under section 104 above, and the weekly rate of the increase exceeds the amount specified in Schedule 4, Part V, paragraph 2(a); and

(b) his need for constant attendance of an extent and nature qualifying him for such an increase at a weekly rate in excess of that amount is likely to be permanent,

the weekly rate of the pension shall, in addition to any increase under section 104 above, be further increased by the amount specified in Schedule 4, Part V, paragraph 3.

Mobility allowance

The benefit is designed to assist those with mobility difficulties, in practise other applicable benefits often appear on the CRB in place of this benefit.

Mobility component of personal independence payment

The mobility component of personal independence payment is designed to cover the additional transportation costs an Injured Person incurs as a result of their disability.

As assessment for the eligibility for this benefit focusses on two issues, the Injured Person's ability to plan a journey and the Injured Person's ability to move around generally The greater the difficulty the Injured Person has with these two functions, the greater the level of benefit paid.

Mobility component of disability living allowance

Disability Living Allowance is being replaced by Personal Independence Payment for persons over the age of 16, it will therefore be a benefit which will appear less frequently on CRBs. Injured Persons in receipt of Disability Living Allowance may see their benefit payments terminated, the DWP are then carrying out assessments to determine the eligibility of Injured Persons for Personal Independence Payment.

As can be seen with these benefits, there is some degree of assessment, either physical or means tested, by which the applicable benefits are awarded. In order to understand the specific details for the award of a particular benefit, a party needs to analyse the Injured Person's DWP records.

CHAPTER THREE
OBTAINING A CERTIFICATE OF RECOVERABLE BENEFITS

To obtain a CRB, the Compensator must register the Injured Person's claim with the CRU, this should be done within 14 days of receiving the details of the claim from the Injured Person or their representative. Registering the claim does not mean that the Compensator is accepting liability for the claim, it only triggers the CRU's involvement in gathering information needed to prepare the necessary certificates to send to the Compensator.

The Compensator does not have any remit to decline to register the claim with the CRU. The obligation to register the claim with the CRU is a statutory one imposed by ***s4(1) Recovery of Benefits Act:***

> *Before a person ("the Compensator") makes a compensation payment he must apply to the Secretary of State for a certificate of recoverable benefits.*

As can be seen the obligation is mandatory. If the Compensator fails to register the claim with the CRU, the Compensator is still liable to repay to the Secretary of State, any benefits listed on the CRB even if the claim has settled. The statutory liability imposed upon the Compensator is not extinguished by the settlement of the claim brought by the Injured Person against the Compensator. The CRU has the power to return to the Compensator post settlement and seek repayment of any applicable benefits listed on the CRB. Pursuant to *s7(3)&(4)* ***Recovery of Benefits Act***, these powers extend to taking civil enforcement action through the Court if the monies are not repaid to the Secretary of State.

The Compensator's liability to the Secretary of State is imposed by statute and therefore the Secretary of State has six years to bring any proceedings to recover any benefits owed by the Compensator. Pursuant to ***s9(1) Limitation Act (1980)***:

> *An action to recover any sum recoverable by virtue of any enactment shall not be brought after the expiration of six years from the date on which the cause of action accrued.*

From a practical perspective, should the Compensator have settled the claim and not registered the matter with the CRU, then the Compensator will have lost the chance to offset those applicable benefits against the corresponding heads of loss sought in the claim. This could potentially leave the Compensator financially prejudiced.

It is a straightforward matter to register a claim with the CRU and the Compensator registers the case by completing and submitting to the CRU form CRU 1. As the reader will observe, various details are required, but not all are applicable to each claim. The full list of information details required by the CRU is set out on the CRU's website; this sets out the following information required:

- *the injured person's full name and address*
- *their date of birth*
- *National Insurance number, if known*
- *the date of the accident, incident or injury*
- *a full description of the nature of the accident, incident, injury or disease*
- *whether the accident was a road traffic accident (RTA) which occurred prior to 29 January 2007*

- *if the person attended an NHS hospital because of the RTA, the injury or the incident on or after 29 January 2007 (at any time for any treatment, examination etc.)*
- *the full name and address of the hospitals or trusts the injured person attended or was admitted to (in order of attendance)*
- *if you are claiming an exemption under the Road Traffic Act (1988) you must state the category of exemption, for RTA's prior to 29 January 2007*
- *whether or not the injured person was employed at the date of incident*
- *where the date of incident is before 6 April 1994, details of the injured person's employment (if known) – this will enable the CRU to obtain information about Statutory Sick Pay (SSP) that may have been paid*
- *the reference number the Compensators uses to identify the case. If the Compensator's reference number changes before the claim is settled, they should inform the CRU of the new reference number*
- *to help the CRU process the claim, please tell the CRU whether the claim is public liability (P), motor (M), employer (E), clinical negligence (C) or other (O)*
- *if a claim is registered as 'M' liability but the accident occurred during a person's employment you must notify the CRU of that fact – this is because the injured person may have claimed Industrial Injuries Disablement Benefit*
- *in 'E' liability cases if SSP was paid before 6 April 1994 the compensator must provide details of the SSP when applying for a Certificate*

- *if a solicitor is acting on the Compensator's behalf they must show their name, address and reference number on form CRU1. This will ensure that correspondence is sent to the correct address*

The information should be provided to the Compensator by the Injured Person/'s representative. Upon receipt of a CRU 1, the CRU start to take steps to gather information and compile a CRB. The CRB will then be issued to the Injured Person and to the Compensator. The CRB will set out the total of each recoverable benefit paid up to a specified date; the total amount of each recoverable lump sum payment paid; the rate expected to be paid for a short future period if benefits are still being paid; confirmation as to whether any of the above amounts or dates have been estimated; the total amount to be repaid to the Secretary of State, and finally the date the CRB ceases to be valid. Some CRB's will also set out the details of the Injured Person's identity and where appropriate the date of the incident that gave rise to the claim for damages.

As can be seen, the CRB may set out a monetary rate of benefits that are expected to be paid in the future. The law allows the CRU to estimate any amount, date or period specified in the CRB, pursuant to *s5(4)* ***Recovery of Benefits Act***:

> *The Secretary of State may estimate, in such manner as he thinks fit, any of the amounts, rates or periods specified in the certificate.*

In addition ***Regulation 9(3)*** of the ***Social Security (Recovery of Benefits) (Lump Sum Payments) Regulations 2008*** provides:

> *The Secretary of State may estimate, in such manner as the Secretary of State thinks fit the amount of the lump sum payments specified in the certificate.*

In urgent circumstances, a CRB can be issued rapidly, but in most cases, and pursuant to *s4(3)(b)* of the ***Recovery of Benefits Act***, the CRB must be issued within four weeks of the Compensator applying for the CRB.

If no benefits have been paid then a 'nil certificate' will be issued, and the parties can be satisfied that issues regarding offsetting and recovering benefits can be put aside for the duration of the CRB. It should be remembered, that the CRB is time limited and certificates often need to be updated during the life of a claim. The content of the certificate may therefore change when it is updated and a new CRB issued. Should a nil CRB be issued then, importantly for the Compensator, the Compensator may settle the claim with the knowledge that there is no issue concerning offsetting of benefits that will impact upon the settlement terms. This is conditional though upon the correct information being provided in the CRU 1.

If the correct information has been provided in the CRU 1 then, during the validity period of the CRB the amount of recoverable benefits cannot be increased. If incorrect or incomplete information has been provided, then the CRU are entitled to review the correct information and issue a revised CRB. A revised CRB could list applicable benefit payments and cause difficulties for the parties in reaching a settlement of the claim.

As experienced practitioners will know, there are occasions where a nil certificate has been issued by the CRU, but when the CRB is updated, the updated certificate shows repayable benefits have been applied. In such circumstances, the CRB should be carefully considered by the Compensator to ensure that the benefits do relate to the claim being brought. Should they be unrelated then the Compensator may wish to consider writing to the CRU asking for a Review of the certificate where appropriate. The issue about Reviewing, seeking a Mandatory Reconsideration and potentially lodging an Appeal of the CRB is addressed in more detail later in this book in a separate chapter.

The CRB is time limited and will expire upon its stated date, it is advisable to ensure that, when making a settlement offer or settling a case, that the CRB is up to date so that parties know what benefits are applicable to the offer and/or settlement. In order to update the CRB, parties can write to the CRU and submit a CRU 4 form requesting an updated certificate. Alternatively, and increasingly the preferred option, Compensators can make use of the CRU's e-service provided through the DWP's website, whereby an updated CRB can be requested online. Compensators and their representatives can use the CRU online e-service for numerous functions these include:

- requesting a certificate for a claim that has already been registered
- notifying the result of a claim that has already been registered
- checking a previous e-service transaction

CHAPTER FOUR
SETTLEMENT OFFERS

The point at which a settlement offer is made in a case is one of the most important phases when applicable benefits have to be considered. When making or receiving an offer of settlement, parties have to consider which recoverable benefits apply to the claim, and how these affect the level of compensation the Injured Person would receive should the offer be accepted. The premise for offsetting applicable benefits is set out in ***McGregor on Damages 20th Ed. 40-221***:

> *it remains necessary, once again, to examine each particular type of collateral benefit separately, although it may be said in advance that the current position is that, in this context,* ***collateral benefits throughout do not operate so as to reduce the damages, with the one clear exception of social security benefits, both monetary and non-monetary****. (emphasis added).*

In certain situations, the applicable benefits can be offset against relevant heads of loss so as to reduce the level of compensation received by the Injured Person and prevent double recovery. It is clearly in the best of interests of the Compensator to ensure that applicable benefits are offset where appropriate to avoid over-compensation being paid.

From the perspective of all parties to the litigation and importantly from the perspective of the Court, it is necessary to ensure that any benefits which the Compensator is seeking to offset against the settlement offer, are clearly set out in that offer. The process of offsetting can be a painstaking process on some cases, as each benefit has to be analysed in turn and checked against the Claimant's Statements of Case and Schedule of Loss, to assess whether it can be offset or not.

The power of the Compensator to offset any applicable benefits derives from ***s8(3) Recovery of Benefits Act***, which provides:

> *For each head of compensation listed in column 1 of the Schedule for which paragraphs (a) and (b) of subsection (1) are met, so much of the gross amount of the compensation payment as is attributable to that head is to be reduced (to nil, if necessary) by deducting the amount of the recoverable benefit or, as the case may be, the aggregate amount of the recoverable benefits shown against it.*

When making and considering offers of settlement in the substantive litigation, the parties should also at this stage consider how they wish to approach any appeal against the CRB as well. An important point for the parties to consider at the offer stage is whether or not they intend to seek to challenge the CRB post settlement of the substantive action. If so, the parties will wish to address at this stage who will retain any monies recovered in an appeal of the CRB.

If the Compensator wishes to retain any monies recovered in an appeal, then there should be an agreement between the parties that the Compensator will retain those monies. This issue is considered in more detail in the CRU Review and Appeals chapter of this book, but it is appropriate for the Compensator to consider the issue at this stage when trying to settle the substantive claim. If there is no agreement that the Compensator will retain the monies, then any monies recovered through a CRU appeal may be returned to the Injured Person. The Compensator will therefore wish to consider whether to agree a term in the settlement conclusion displacing that position.

When addressing state benefits in settlement offers, the parties need to be clear in the offer as to their intentions in relation to those benefits, and how they are being treated in the offer. The importance of clear drafting in an offer is underlined by the Court of Appeal's judgment in ***Rees v West Glamorgan [1994] P.I.Q.R. P37***, readers will note that the judgment pre-dates the current recovery scheme and indeed the implementation of the Civil Procedure Rules and thus Part 36 offers. It remains to be tested as to whether the judgment survives the implementation of the current CRU scheme. The judgment provides that if the parties intend to make an agreement whereby the statutory deduction of benefits is not to be made, then that had to be agreed expressly in the offer correspondence. Failing to do otherwise means that the deduction is to be made from the offer.

As such, a settlement offer will be gross of CRU deductions unless stated otherwise, and an Offeree will not wish to be caught out by advising their client of a settlement figure, only to have to later give further advice, and advise the Injured Person that they will be receiving less compensation owing to applicable benefits being deducted.

Types of settlement offer

When the Offeror drafts their offer, they need to consider the CRB and assess what benefits are contained on it. Clearly if the CRB shows nil benefits then there is no issue about offsetting to consider. If the CRB does set out benefits then the Offeror needs to consider how those benefits affect the settlement offer.

The manner by which the Offeror goes about addressing the offsetting issues depends upon the format of the offer being made. The substantive claim can be settled in a number of different ways and it is therefore important to identify what type of offer is being made before the Offeror can decide how the CRB affects that offer.

There are three common methods by which claims are settled, and they will each be considered in turn. The first method is a Calderbank offer; the second method is an offer that complies with Part 36 of the Civil Procedure Rules; thirdly, parties may settle a claim at a Joint Settlement Meeting ('JSM'). Howsoever the settlement is approached, and as set out above, the Offeror needs to ensure that the settlement terms are clearly laid out for the Offeree to understand. Lack of clarity can cause complications later on and may lead to a Court having to determine a dispute as to the settlement provisions. This can be costly and time consuming, as well as deprive a party who thought they were secure in their position of that security.

Calderbank offers

Calderbank offers have been permissible in civil litigation since the case of ***Calderbank v Calderbank [1975] 3 All ER 333 (EWCA)***. This case introduced the concept of a settlement offer being made 'without prejudice save as to costs', this means that if the offer is not accepted, it cannot be referred to during the course of the proceedings, but it can be referred to the court on the question of costs.

This chapter is not designed to discuss the pros and cons of making a Calderbank offer as opposed to a Part 36 offer, but Calderbank offers may be used as an alternative to Part 36 offers. If an Offeror is making a Part 36 offer then they must comply with the strict requirements of Part 36 of the Civil Procedure Rules, there is no corresponding rule by which an Offeror making a Calderbank offer must comply. Calderbank offers therefore permit a greater degree of flexibility than Part 36 offers, for example, a Calderbank offer can vary issues such as the time period for which the offer is open and the timescales for payment, and this can have advantages in certain situations.

Whilst a Calderbank offer provides greater flexibility in how the offer can be termed, the costs consequences that flow from such an offer are not as well prescribed as those which flow from a well-placed Part 36 offer, and are very much at the discretion of the Court. The costs consequences that flow from a well-pitched Part 36 offer are strict, and are set out by the Civil Procedure Rules, for example CPR 36.17.

As the reader can therefore appreciate, there are various considerations and trade-offs between the two offers, and an Offeror needs to consider when deciding which form of offer is most appropriate to the case before them. This will inevitably turn on the particular circumstances of each case.

Given the flexibility afforded to an Offeror when drafting a Calderbank offer, the Offeror can set out in the offer how the benefits listed on the CRB are being offset, if at all. It must be remembered that a Compensator may not necessarily seek to offset any benefits listed on the CRB and may choose to either repay these to the CRU in full or seek to appeal to the CRU in relation to those benefits. These considerations need to be addressed by the Offeror when making the settlement offer, and will vary depending on the circumstances of each claim.

If a Calderbank offer is being made, then the position about offsetting CRU benefits is governed exclusively by the terms of the offer, clear drafting in the offer is therefore vital to ensure that each party, the CRU, and should their intervention be required, the Court, can see what the true intention of the offer is.

Whilst not directly analogous or required, the clear terminology required by Part 36 of the Civil Procedure Rules can provide helpful guidance to an Offeror when drafting its settlement offer. Part 36 is discussed in more detail below but briefly, the rule requires that when making its offer the Compensator must address the following issues in its offer:

1. The gross amount of the offer being made before any deductions are taken into consideration

2. The name of any deductible benefit on the CRB and the amount of the deduction

3. The net amount of the offer after any and all of the CRU deductions have been made

When making a Calderbank offer, the Offeror may therefore wish to consider those requirements, to help them to lay out in clear and logical terms, the offer and the settlement figures being put to the Offeree. If the above principles are followed then the Offeree can see what figure is being offered as a gross sum, what benefits are being applied to the Calderbank offer, the amount of the deductions, and lastly what figure the Offeree is receiving after the applied benefits have been offset.

Part 36 offers

If the Offeror makes a settlement offer pursuant to Part 36 of the Civil Procedure Rules then ***CPR 36.22*** governs the issue of the deduction of benefits and lump sum payments. The first position to consider is, pursuant to ***CPR 36.22(3)(a)&(b)***, whether the offer is made without regard to CRU benefits or is intended to take account of CRU benefits. This rule provides:

> *(3) A defendant who makes a Part 36 offer must, where relevant, state either—*
>
> *(a) that the offer is made without regard to any liability for recoverable amounts; or*
>
> *(b) that it is intended to include any deductible amounts.*

If the offer is not intended to take account of recoverable benefits then clearly no consideration need be given to deduction of benefits, the Offeror should state this clearly in the Part 36 offer, and thereafter outline the figure for compensation being offered in settlement of the claim.

If the offer is intended to take account of deductible benefits, then sections *(5)* to *(9)* inclusive of ***CPR 36.22*** need to be considered. The starting point is ***CPR 36.22(5)***, which provides that the Offeror has to apply for a CRB before making a Part 36 offer:

> *(5) Before making the Part 36 offer, the offeror must apply for a certificate.*

As can be seen, the prerequisite to making the Part 36 offer is that the Offeror needs to have applied for a CRB, readers will note that that the requirement is only for a certificate to have been applied for, not actually received. As will be recalled from the third chapter of this book, the claim should be registered with the CRU at the outset, and the CRB should therefore be received by the time a settlement offer is made.

If at the time the Offeror makes the Part 36 offer, the Offeror has not received a CRB, then pursuant to ***CPR 36.22(7)***, the Offeror must clarify the offer by stating the name and amount of any deductible amounts by which the gross amount is reduced; and the net amount of compensation. This information must be provided not more than 7 days after receipt of the Certificate. ***CPR 36.22(7)*** states:

> *(7) If at the time the offeror makes the Part 36 offer, the offeror has applied for, but has not received, a certificate, the offeror must clarify the offer by stating the matters referred to in paragraph (6)(b) and (c) not more than 7 days after receipt of the certificate.*

As can be seen, the provision is mandatory, readers will note the terminology '***must***' (emphasis added) required by the Rule. The provision allows an Offeror to make an offer to settle at a time when he has applied for but not received a CRB, and which will have the consequences of a Part 36 offer. The specified condition of confirming the deductible amounts and the net amount must be complied with to achieve the costs protection and consequences afforded to a well-placed

Part 36 offer. There is no authority to establish the effect of non-compliance with this rule, but the mandatory requirement for compliance would indicate that a failure to comply with this provision could potentially render the Part 36 offer nugatory if the Offeror breaches ***CPR 36.22(7)***. This is a point however that has, so far, not been tested, save that the court held in ***Momonakaya v the Ministry of Defence*** *[2019] EWHC 480 (QB)* that a de minimis breach of the sub rules did not invalidate the Part 36 offer.

Where a CRB is obtained and recoverable benefits are shown on the certificate, then, as set out at ***CPR 36.22(6)*** the Part 36 offer must address three issues:

> *(a) the gross amount of compensation;*
>
> *(b) the name and amount of any deductible amounts by which the gross amount is reduced; and*
>
> *(c) the net amount of compensation.*

The reasoning for this is clear, in that it provides clarity to both the Offeror and Offeree, and enables them to consider, advise and know exactly what settlement figures are being offered. Should any dispute, arise it also provides the necessary information to allow the Court to determine the dispute and assess what was being offered to settle the claim.

If the Offeror is making a Part 36 offer then many practitioners use the standard form to make Part 36 offers, this provides a box for the Offeror to set out its position in relation to the CRB and any offsets being made.

Joint settlement meeting

In many larger multi track cases, but not all of them, parties may settle the claim at a JSM. Should the parties to a case settle the claim at a JSM, then there is the opportunity to agree at the meeting as to how any applicable benefits will be offset, if at all.

There is usually no formal written offer of settlement passing between the parties at such meetings, and settlement is reached on a verbal basis. The agreed settlement terms are often embodied in a settlement agreement or, if Court proceedings have been commenced, embodied in a Consent Order or Tomlin Order that sets out the agreed settlement terms, this is then filed at Court. The parties can therefore write into the agreed settlement terms the details of how, if at all, CRU deductions are accounted for and how any appeal against the CRB is to be approached.

Trials

Whilst of course resolution of a case at trial is not a resolution by way of settlement offer, if the substantive litigation is resolved at trial, then the Court order must set out what, if any benefits are being deducted from the compensation payment being ordered, pursuant to ***s15 Recovery Benefits Act***:

(1) *This section applies where a court makes an order for a compensation payment to be made in any case, unless the order is made with the consent of the injured person and the person by whom the payment is to be made.*

(2) *The court must, in the case of each head of compensation listed in column 1 of Schedule 2 to which any of the compensation payment is attributable, specify in the order the amount of the compensation payment which is attributable to that head.*

CHAPTER FIVE
OFFSETTING BENEFITS AND COSTS CONSEQUENCES

As readers will recall from the second chapter, there are various benefits that may be listed on a CRB, but those benefits can only be offset against certain heads of damage. A key part of the enactment of the Recovery of Benefits Act was to ensure that benefits can only be deducted on a "like for like" basis; that is to say that an applicable benefit can only be offset against an equivalent head of compensation. When making a settlement offer, the Offeror needs to be clear which benefits are being offset against which heads of damage, and it must be ensured that the settlement offer does not try to offset benefits against non-corresponding heads of compensation.

The heads of compensation and applicable benefits table is set out in *Schedule 2 Recovery of Benefits Act*. This provides:

Head of Compensation	Benefit
1. Compensation for earnings lost during the relevant period.	a) Universal credit b) Disablement pension payable under section 103 of the 1992 Act c) Employment and support allowance d) Incapacity benefit e) Income support f) Invalidity pension and allowance g) Jobseeker's allowance

	h) Reduced earnings allowance i) Severe disablement allowance j) Sickness benefit k) Unemployability supplement l) Unemployment benefit
2. Compensation for cost of care incurred during the relevant period.	a) Attendance allowance b) Daily living component of personal independence payment c) Care component of disability living allowance d) Disablement pension increase payable under section 104 or 105 of the 1992 Act
3. Compensation for loss of mobility during the relevant period.	a) Mobility allowance b) Mobility component of personal independence payment c) Mobility component of disability living allowance

A brief discussion of these benefits took place in the second chapter of this book. As readers will note there is no provision for benefits to be offset against pain, suffering and loss of amenity, as these damages are 'ring fenced' and cannot be altered by CRU benefits. When calculating the net offer being made, the Offeror has to ignore the impact of the CRB on pain, suffering and loss of amenity. This rule was underlined by the Court of Appeal in ***Williams v Devon CC [2003] EWCA Civ 365***. The position in relation to non-ring-fenced damages in lump sum scheme cases is addressed below.

In some cases, a claim may not have been made for loss of earnings, costs of care and/or loss of mobility and there is therefore no head of damage to offset the benefits against. In these circumstances, a Compensator cannot offset benefits listed in another column against a head of damage in order to reduce their liability. If the benefits listed on the CRB cannot be offset against the claimed head of damage, then the Compensator has to pay the benefits to the CRU in the first instance and then apply for a Review, Mandatory Reconsideration and/or Appeal the Certificate to the CRB. This is just one of the reasons it is important to consider at the stage when the offer is made, who will retain any monies recovered in a CRU appeal.

Relevant period

There is a 'cut off period' for the accrual of benefits, and this can reduce a Compensator's liability in long running claims. The starting point in this regard is ***s6(1) Recovery of Benefits Act*** which provides:

> *A person who makes a compensation payment in any case is liable to pay to the Secretary of State an amount equal to the total amount of the recoverable benefits.*

Prima facie, the Compensator must therefore repay the whole of the benefits. This position is tempered slightly by the application of ***s1 Recovery of Benefits Act***, which provides that the Act applies where:

i. *a person makes a payment (whether on his own behalf or not) to or in respect of any other person in consequence of any accident, injury or disease suffered by the other, and*

ii. *any listed benefits have been, or are likely to be, paid to or for the other during the relevant period in respect of the accident, injury or disease.*

The Compensator is therefore liable to account to the Secretary of State for benefits paid during the 'relevant period', ***s3(2) Recovery of Benefits Act*** defines the 'relevant period' as:

> *Subject to subsection (4), if it is a case of accident or injury, the relevant period is the period of five years immediately following the day on which the accident or injury in question occurred.*

This rule can be easily applied in a claim where, for example, the Injured Person falls at work and sustains an injury in an accident where there is a clearly identifiable accident date. The rule is somewhat more difficult to apply in claims arising for industrial disease where there is no easily identifiable date of accident. If a claim has been made for benefits because of a disease, the CRU's Technical Guidance Note sets out that the amount the Compensator has to pay is calculated from the day the injured party first claimed a benefit because of the disease, up to the date of the final compensation payment, or for up to five years, whichever is earlier.

Examples

The previous chapter, and the above sections, set out the law governing how to approach the requirements of making valid settlement offers and how the benefits can be offset against heads of damage being claimed. The next section looks at some practical examples as to how this works when offers of settlement are made. All of the examples assume that the Compensator is seeking to deduct the applicable benefits from the claim advanced by the Injured Person.

Example 1

Take a personal injury case where the Injured Person sustained an injury at work. Following the accident the CRB shows payments of Universal Credit ('UC') benefits of £5,000. The Claimant's Schedule of Loss seeks a sum of £10,000 for the Claimant's loss of earnings.

If a Compensator makes a Part 36 offer of £25,000 then the net figure offered to the Claimant will be £20,000, ie. the £25,000 gross offer minus the £5,000 for UC benefits which can be offset against the loss of earnings claimed in the Schedule of Loss.

The above example is a very simplistic one and is the most basic scenario that a practitioner will probably encounter. The following examples set out some more in depth scenarios encountered in calculating offsets.

Example 2

Take another personal injury case. Following the accident, the CRB bears payments of UC benefits of £5,000 and Daily Living Component of Personal Independence Payment (DLCPIP) benefits of £2,000. The Schedule of Loss seeks a sum of £10,000 for the Claimant's loss of earnings and £3,000 for care.

If a Defendant makes a Part 36 Offer of £25,000 then the net figure offered to the Claimant will be £18,000, ie. the £25,000 gross offer minus the £5,000 for UC benefits which can be offset against the loss of earnings, and the £2,000 which can be offset against the DLCPIP benefits claimed in the Schedule of Loss.

The above examples give practitioners a view of offsets in a case involving one category of applicable benefit, and a case involving a multi benefit CRB. Both of the examples set out situations where the losses claimed are higher than the amounts claimed in the CRB.

The following examples involve cases where the benefits on the CRB are higher than the amounts claimed in the Schedule of Loss and are more complex.

Example 3

Take another personal injury case. Following the accident, the CRB bears payments of UC benefits of £5,000 and DLCPIP benefits of £2,000. The Schedule of Loss seeks a sum of £10,000 for the Claimant's loss of earnings only.

If a Defendant makes a Part 36 Offer of £25,000 then the net figure offered to the Claimant will be £20,000, ie. the £25,000 gross offer minus the £5,000 for UC benefits which can be offset against the loss of earnings claimed in the Schedule of Loss.

There is no claim for damages against which the DLCPIP benefits can be offset. The Compensator therefore cannot offset those benefits against any head of loss and must repay them to the Secretary of State.

Example 4

Take another personal injury case. Following the accident, the CRB bears payments of UC benefits of £15,000 and DLCPIP benefits of £2,000. The Schedule of Loss seeks a sum of £10,000 for the Claimant's loss of earnings and £1,000 for care.

If a Defendant makes a Part 36 Offer of £25,000 then the net figure offered to the Claimant will be £14,000, ie. the £25,000 gross offer minus the £10,000 for UC benefits which can be offset against the loss of earnings claimed in the Schedule of Loss and the £1,000 for which the DLCPIP benefits can be offset.

Whilst the Claimant has advanced a claim for loss of earnings, against which the UC benefits can be offset, the claim does not cover the entirety of the benefits listed on the CRB and the Compensator must therefore repay the balance to the Secretary of State.

Interest

An issue that has required some intervention from the appellate Courts is the question of how to address calculations for interest. In this regard, the starting point is the judgment of the House of Lords in the linked appeals of ***Wisely v John Fulton (Plumbers) Ltd and Wadey v Surrey County Council [2000] 1 WLR 820***. Here it was held that an Injured Person is entitled to recover interest in respect of damages covered by benefit payments.

The issue of how that interest is then treated for the purposes of off-setting against the settlement sums then has to be considered. If an Injured Person receives recoverable benefits that exceed the amount that they are awarded in damages, the interest awarded on the damages can be taken into consideration when offsetting the benefits from the damages awarded.

This issue was examined by the Court in the cases of ***Re: British Coal Respiratory Disease Litigation [2000] All ER (D) 1552*** (which was later upheld on appeal ***Griffiths and others v British Coal Corporation and another [2001] EWCA Civ 336***). It was held that, while the rate of interest might reflect the loss of use of the money for the relevant period, it was not unjust, when benefits exceeded the total of damage, that an Injured Person be required to bring into account against the applicable benefit, that interest sum which had been calculated.

Lump sum payments

Applicable benefits can also be recovered from damages awarded pursuant to compensation schemes established to assist workers suffering from diseases contracted during their working lifetime. Lump sum payments recoverable under the Recovery of Benefits Act include those made under:

- the Pneumoconiosis etc. (Workers' Compensation) Act 1979
- the 2008 Diffuse Mesothelioma Scheme
- the 2014 Diffuse Mesothelioma Payment Scheme
- any ex-statutory payment that was paid because the person did not qualify for a payment under the 1979 Act

Lumps sum payments can also be made under Part 4 of the ***Child Maintenance and Other Payments Act 2008***, which relates to diffuse mesothelioma claims. It is not intended to set out in detail the provisions of each scheme as this is outside the remit of this book, the schemes operate to pay a lump sum to successful applicants. The important point to note for the purposes of offsetting when considering CRU issues touching on this scheme, is that where a compensation award is reduced to take account of lump sum recoveries, the Compensator must reduce the general damages element of the compensation award before reducing any of the special damages element of the award.

This is contrasted with the rule in ***Williams v Devon*** (discussed earlier and set out above) where general damages are ring fenced. The rule for lump sum deductions in these schemes derives from ***Reg 12(6) Social Security (Recovery of Benefits) (Lump Sum Payments) (2008)*** which provides:

(6) The reduction specified in paragraph (3) is to be attributed to the heads of compensation in the following order—

(a) damages for non-pecuniary loss;

(b) damages for pecuniary loss,

Therefore, when approaching the calculations of offsetting for lump sum payments and benefit recovery, if an award of £50,000 had been made and comprised of £20,000 for general damages and £30,000 for loss of earnings, if the CRB listed lump sum payments totalling £35,000 for Incapacity Benefit, the Compensator must offset the £20,000 lump sum payment from the general damages first. This would leave an outstanding balance of £15,000. An offset may then be applied to any of the remaining heads of compensation. The Compensator can then offset the remaining £15,000 listed on the CRB against the Incapacity Benefit, leaving the Injured Person with £15,000 in compensation.

Costs consequences of settlement offers

The above sections address how settlement offers can be made, and how applicable benefits may be deducted from those offers. Settlement offers can of course remain in effect for much or all of the life of the litigation, and may need to be considered by a Court should a case be resolved at trial. An Offeror does not always make a settlement offer solely to try to settle the claim, but to also provide protection in relation to the costs of the Offeree should the offer not be accepted.

A complicating factor in settling claims is how a party or ultimately the Court approaches a situation where further benefits have accrued since the time a Part 36 offer was made and the case reaching a resolution. The issue over whether an Injured Person has obtained a more advantageous settlement than what was offered by the Offeror in the settlement offer can cause complications in a case.

If an Offeror has made a Part 36 offer then the parties and the Court have to consider ***CPR 36.22(8)&(9)***, these provide:

> *(8) For the purposes of rule 36.17(1)(a), a claimant fails to recover more than any sum offered (including a lump sum offered under rule 36.6) if the claimant fails upon judgment being entered to recover a sum, once deductible amounts identified in the judgment have been deducted, greater than the net amount stated under paragraph (6)(c). (Section 15(2) of the 1997 Act provides that the court must specify the compensation payment attributable to each head of damage. Schedule 1 to the 2008 Regulations modifies section 15 of the 1997 Act in relation to lump sum payments and provides that the court must specify the compensation payment attributable to each or any dependant who has received a lump sum payment.)*
>
> *(9) Where—*
>
> *(a) further deductible amounts have accrued since the Part 36 offer was made; and*
>
> *(b) the court gives permission to accept the Part 36 offer, the court may direct that the amount of the offer payable to the offeree shall be reduced by a sum equivalent to the deductible amounts paid to the claimant since the date of the offer.*
>
> *(Rule 36.11(3)(b) states that permission is required to accept an offer where the relevant period has expired and further deductible amounts have been paid to the claimant.)*

The issue is addressed by the Court of Appeal in the leading authority of ***Colin Crooks v Hendricks Lovell Limited [2016] EWCA Civ 1848***. This issue can be of great significance to a claim between the parties, and substantial costs may be at stake should the situation arise, as such the judgment is addressed in some detail below.

By way of background, in this case the Injured Person brought a claim for personal injury and loss arising from an accident at work in 2009. Liability was admitted but issues of medical causation remained. By the time the claim reached trial the Injured Person's claim for special damages was £184,674 of which almost £183,000 represented past and future lost earnings. The parties were considerably apart in terms of medical evidence and this was reflected by their respective Part 36 offers.

In September 2012, the Compensator made a Part 36 offer to the Injured Person in the sum of £18,500 using the standard form N242A. The offer was stated to be inclusive of interim payments amounting to £18,500 and crucially was stated to be made *"net of CRU"*. The offer also stated (in another part of the form) that it was made *"without regard to any liability for recoverable benefits"*. In October 2013, the Injured Person made a Part 36 offer of £47,500 *"net of CRU and inclusive of interim payments"*. This offer was withdrawn shortly before trial and it was the effect of the Compensator's offer of September 2012, which was to be considered in the Court's judgment.

A CRB covering the trial on 14 and 15 November 2013 showed recoverable benefits of £16,262.76. Giving judgment on 15 November, the Recorder attributed only 12 months' lost earnings to the accident. He awarded the Injured Person a total sum of £29,550, comprising £4,000 for PSLA, £25,500 for past loss of earnings and £50 for miscellaneous expenses. However, because the Injured Person had indicated his intention to launch a formal review of the CRB, the Recorder adjourned his consideration of costs, and therefore the question of whether the Injured Person had beaten the Compensator's Part 36 offer, until the outcome of the review of the CRB.

The review was partially successful so that a new sum of £6,760.11 was capable of being offset against the Injured Person's damages. The Recorder held that the Injured Person had failed to better the Compensator's Part 36 offer and made an order for costs in favour of the Compensator from the last date for acceptance of the Part 36 offer. In doing so, he had accepted the Compensator's argument that broadly went as follows:

- Before the review of the CRB the value of the offer was £18,500 plus the benefits of £16,262.76 making a total of £34,762.76 and therefore, in the absence of the review, the Injured Person's award was £5,212.76 less than the offer.

- After the review of the CRB, the value of the offer was £18,500 plus recoverable benefits of £6,760.11, plus £9,502.65 from the CRU refund to be paid to the Injured Person. This made a total of £34,762.76 and the Injured Person's award was still £5,212.76 less than the offer.

The Injured Person appealed contending that he should not be liable for the Compensator's costs. The Court of Appeal had to address three issues: first, whether the Recorder misconstrued the Compensator's Part 36 offer, misdirecting himself as to the meaning of the words *"net of CRU"*. Secondly, whether the rules required him to consider the costs of the action at the conclusion of the trial, rather than awaiting the outcome of the review of the CRB. Thirdly, whether the Recorder was wrong to award costs in favour of the Compensator.

The Court of Appeal allowed the appeal and reversed the Recorder's decision holding that the Injured Person was not liable to pay the Compensator's costs after expiry of the Part 36 offer. Each of the questions faced by the Court of Appeal is addressed as follows:

Did the Recorder misconstrue the Compensator's Part 36 offer?

The offer was held to be a valid Part 36 offer. The crucial point was the meaning of the expression *"net of CRU"*. When an offer is stated to be "net of", in this case CRU, it must be read as having been made without regard to liability for recoverable benefits. In the context of the case before the Recorder, that must therefore mean that the sum of £18,500 would not be reduced by the recoverable benefits.

Was the Recorder right to adjourn his consideration of the costs position until the outcome of the review?

It was appropriate for the Recorder to await the result of the review before determining whether the Injured Person had beaten the Part 36 offer. Pursuant to what was then CPR 36.14, it was not appropriate for the Recorder to proceed straight away to determine the issue of costs. The rule, as it then was (the rule numbers have since changed but the substance remains the same) provided that:

> *CPR 36.14 Costs consequences following judgment*
>
> *(1) This rule applies where upon judgment being entered –*
>
> *(a) a claimant fails to obtain a judgment more advantageous than a defendant's Part 36 offer; or*
>
> *(b) judgment against the defendant is at least as advantageous to the claimant as the proposals contained in a claimant's Part 36 offer.*

On the basis that not all of the relevant circumstances had occurred at the time judgment was given, and the correct amount of recoverable benefits still required determination, it was not appropriate for the Recorder to move straight on to consider the issue of where the costs liability lay, and the Recorder was right to adjourn matters.

Did the Injured Person beat the Compensator's Part 36 offer?

The Recorder was wrong to conclude that the Injured Person had failed to beat the Compensator's offer as he ultimately obtained a more advantageous result than the Part 36 offer. When determining whether the Compensator had beaten the Part 36 offer, it was necessary to compare the offer with the judgment award on the same basis, allowing for any necessary subtraction of the figures for CRU from the total figure for damages.

The approach the Recorder should have taken was to consider the effect of the CRU's review decision on the composition of the judgment award once the final CRU figure was incorporated. He had been wrong to look at the matter in terms of the amounts paid by the Compensator. What he should have done was look at whether the total payment the Injured Person would actually receive was more or less than the amount of the offer. Had he done so he would have acknowledged that this left the Injured Person receiving a higher figure than the Compensator's Part 36 offer and therefore a more advantageous judgment. On 15 November 2013, the amount payable to the Injured Person net of benefits would have been £13,287.24. After the review, the amount payable to the Injured Person net of benefits was £22,789.89 therefore beating the £18,500 offer.

Accordingly the Compensator was ordered to pay the Injured Person's costs of the proceedings.

The Court of Appeal's decision in relation to the first point brings some clarity to the issue of the phrasing of Part 36 offers and emphasises that clear drafting is vitally important when setting out deductions to be made from settlement offers. This point is particularly important to litigants as the Compensator had made its offer on the standard form N242A, the use of which is now much more common, and the clarification from the Court should be welcomed as assisting the parties in interpreting offers clearly.

It is however, the third issue that is the most significant aspect of the judgment. Cases that have relatively modest values in damages, but a substantial CRB value, are often problematic. This is because the value of the benefits can sometimes impede the settlement, and the judgment does make matters slightly more difficult for Compensators.

First, there will be a delay in obtaining the final order following a trial if the CRB is going to be reviewed or appealed if the offer is made net of recoverable benefits. The Court of Appeal held that, on the second issue, the Recorder was correct to proceed as he did and await the result of the CRU review before making his costs order. This inevitably builds a delay into the case with the parties having to await the CRU's review decision, and also results in a situation where a partial judgment is handed down, but the parties do not yet have finality to the litigation. It can be seen from the chronology of the case that the Recorder gave judgment on 15 November 2013 but the decision on costs was not delivered until 17 October 2014. This delay in bringing about finality to the case does not assist either party in moving on from the litigation. This is a disincentive of making offers net of recoverable benefits as opposed to gross.

Secondly, if the Compensator wishes to make an offer net of recoverable benefits then it now has the added uncertainty that in order to truly compare the final judgment with the Part 36 offer, the CRU's decision must be second-guessed in order to calculate what the final award will be. This places more pressure on Compensator to try to work out what benefits may not be attributable to the accident related injuries and makes calculation of a well-placed net offer more difficult for the Compensator. In practical terms, if a net offer is made at the outset of a piece of ligation when the Compensator may not necessarily have its expert evidence in place, the Compensator may not be aware of what aspects of the CRB may be open to challenge, thus restricting the ability to accurately pitch any net offer. This uncertainty will only make the Compensator's task of making any net offer more difficult.

Drawing on the Court of Appeal's judgment in ***Fox v Foundation Piling Ltd [2011] EWCA Civ 790***, the Court considered that the point of whether an offer has been beaten or not is not something that should be looked at from any complex philosophical perspective but from a common sense point of view. The Injured Person's claim for special damages alone stood at almost £185,000 at the time of trial, but having recovered £29,550, the Injured Person was still awarded his costs. To make such a reduction in the claim but still be liable for the costs may seem unfair to Compensators, but the Court of Appeal reiterated comments from previous decisions that reducing an inflated claim will not necessarily result in a costs order being made against the Compensator. The court reminded practitioners that in such situations:

> "*The defendant's remedy is to make a modest Part 36 offer", and [if] the defendant fails to make a sufficient Part 36 offer at the first opportunity, it cannot expect to secure costs protection*".

The judgment therefore not only serves to bring clarity to the issue of terminology of offers and calculation of final awards, but also as a reminder to Compensators that reducing a claim substantially, but not to such a level that the final award is less than the Compensator's Part 36 offer, will not necessarily yield a costs order against the Injured Person.

The Court of Appeal's judgment builds on the previous judgment of ***McCaffery v Datta (Costs) [1997] 1 W.L.R. 870***, readers should note that the judgment in this case was handed down on 11 December 1996, and as such pre-dates the current CRU scheme. By way of background, the Injured Person was awarded damages in excess of, what was then, a payment into court, but did not personally receive them as they were repaid to the CRU. The Compensator disputed that they therefore had a liability for the Injured Person's costs.

The Court held that the Injured Person may still recover costs, although the Injured Person had personally failed to recover any money in excess of that paid to the CRU, the situation was similar to a subrogated action. The Compensator could not be said to have had been successful as they were still making a payment of damages, just not necessarily to the Injured Person. As can be seen from the perspective of the Compensator, they need to consider at the stage when a settlement offer is made, not only how the benefits can be offset, but what costs protection through to and including a trial and/or appeal the terms of their settlement offer will afford them.

CHAPTER SIX
INTERIM PAYMENTS OF DAMAGES

Issues regarding CRBs do not arise only at the commencement of a claim and upon its conclusion, the impact of the CRB must also be considered at interlocutory stages. Should the Compensator make an interim payment of damages, or if the Injured Person formally applies to Court for an interim payment of damages, then the parties need to assess how the CRB impacts upon the interim payment being made, or ordered.

This chapter analyses the considerations for a Compensator and the obligations placed upon them, when making interim payments of damages either on a voluntary basis, or upon the order of the Court. Lastly, the chapter also analyses how interim payments affect the final judgment sums made at the conclusion of the substantive claim for personal injury brought against the Compensator.

When making an interim payment of damages, the Compensator's liability to repay the recoverable benefits to the Secretary of State is triggered. This does not necessarily mean that benefits cease to accrue at that stage, and should the damages payment only be made on an interim basis and the substantive litigation continue, the Compensator should apply for a fresh CRB, as further applicable benefits may be noted.

Voluntary interim payments of damages

In claims for more substantial levels of damages, it is not uncommon to see requests made by the Injured Person for a voluntary interim payment of damages in order to assist with matters such as rehabilitation treatment or accommodation costs for example. If liability has been admitted or found by a Court at a split trial, the Compensator will often (but not always) voluntarily make a payment on account of damages. Should such a payment be made then the Compensator has to consider its liability to the CRU in relation to benefits listed on the CRB.

If the Compensator voluntarily makes an interim payment, then the CRB must be discharged at that time and the benefits must be repaid to the Secretary of State. If a Compensator makes an interim payment then they are liable to pay the CRU all of the recoverable benefits that the Injured Person has received, up to the date of the interim payment. As readers will recall from chapter one, ***s6(1) Recovery of Benefits Act*** requires the Compensator to pay an amount equal to the total amount of the recoverable benefits, to the Secretary of State when a compensation payment is paid.

The CRB therefore needs to be reviewed to see what benefits are listed on it, the dates of the payment of those benefits and when the interim payment was made. The Compensator can then calculate what amount is due to be repaid to the CRU at the time of the interim payment. Whether any of the applicable benefits are offset against the interim payment will be a matter for the Compensator and Injured Person to agree between themselves in the course of negotiating the voluntary interim payment.

Applications for interim payments of damages

If an agreement cannot be reached between the parties for an interim payment to be made, then the Injured Person has the option to apply formally to Court for an order for an interim payment to be made. In order to obtain an interim payment of damages, the Injured Person must satisfy the requirements of ***CPR 25.7***. There are numerous sections to the test, and it is not proposed to set them all out in this text, the principle considerations in ***CPR 25.7*** are:

> *(1) The court may only make an order for an interim payment where any of the following conditions are satisfied –*
>
> *(a) the defendant against whom the order is sought has admitted liability to pay damages or some other sum of money to the claimant;*
>
> *(b) the claimant has obtained judgment against that defendant for damages to be assessed or for a sum of money (other than costs) to be assessed;*
>
> *(c) it is satisfied that, if the claim went to trial, the claimant would obtain judgment for a substantial amount of money (other than costs) against the defendant from whom he is seeking an order for an interim payment whether or not that defendant is the only defendant or one of a number of defendants to the claim;*

When considering the application, in essence the Court must consider whether the Compensator is going to be liable to pay some level of damages to the Injured Person. In cases where liability is admitted, or where judgment has been entered against the Compensator, the Injured Person will clearly be on better ground subject to the content of the medical evidence in support of the claim.

In all circumstances the Court, when determining the level of any award of damages, will be guided by the evidence relied upon by the parties in support of their positions on causation, loss and damage. Ultimately, the Court has a wide level of discretion when determining an appropriate figure for an interim payment.

If such an application is made, then the Court must take account of the level of the CRB. ***CPR 25.7(5)(b)*** provides that the Court must take into account:

(b) any relevant set-off or counterclaim.

The applicable benefits are, by their very nature, a 'relevant set-off' and must therefore be taken into consideration at this stage. Should the application for an interim payment of damages be successful, and the Court have to determine the level of the award, then the interaction between the level of the interim payment of damages and the CRB is governed by Practice Direction ***CPR 25B PD.4***. This provides that:

> *4.1 Where in a claim for personal injuries there is an application for an interim payment of damages:*
>
> *(a) which is other than by consent;*
>
> *(b) which either:*
>
> *(1) falls under the heads of damage set out in column 1 of Schedule 2 to the Social Security (Recovery of Benefits) Act 1997 ("the 1997 Act") in respect of recoverable benefits received by the claimant set out in column 2 of that Schedule; or*
>
> *(ii) includes damages in respect of a disease for which a lump sum payment within the definition in section 1A(2) of the 1997 Act has been, or is likely to be made; and*
>
> *(c) where the defendant is liable to pay a recoverable amount (as defined in rule 36.15(1)(c)) to the Secretary of State, the defendant should obtain from the Secretary of State a certificate (as defined in rule 36.15(1)(e)).*
>
> *4.2 A copy of the certificate must be filed at the hearing of the application for an interim payment.*
>
> *4.3 The order will set out the deductible amount (as defined in rule 36.15(1)(d)).*

4.4 *The payment made to the claimant will be the net amount but the interim payment for the purposes of paragraph 5 below will be the gross amount.*

So what does all of that mean? Firstly, readers will note that the Practice Direction only applies to applications made other than by consent. Therefore, it is not applicable to cases where the Injured Person issues an application and a compromise is reached before the application is heard. The Practice Direction applies to applications that are contested by the parties, and which require the Court to determine the issues and make an order.

In these cases, the Court has to deduct the applicable benefits from the gross interim payment of damages awarded when making the order at the hearing. A not infrequent consideration for Compensators is therefore whether they wish to contest the application to a hearing, in order to ensure that the applicable benefits are deducted from the interim payment.

Readers will also note that it is mandatory for a copy of the CRB to have been obtained and filed with the Court for the application hearing. Understandably, the Judge will need to see what benefits, if any, need to be deducted from the interim payment award. A copy of the CRB will therefore need to form part of the application papers.

Once the application is heard and the Court order is issued, the Compensator will be able to see what amounts it has a liability to pay to the Injured Person by way of interim payment, and what sums are required to be paid to the Secretary of State for the purposes of discharging the CRB at that stage.

The provisions to offset benefits in accordance with ***Schedule 2 Recovery of Benefits Act***, which was discussed in previous chapters, still exist at the interim payment stage and parties should be mindful as to whether the interim payment sought is calculated according to any of the heads of loss, which are capable of being offset under the Schedule. Readers will also recall the provisions of ***s15 Recovery Benefits Act*** discussed in chapter four requiring the Court order under which the award for damages is made, to set out what, if any benefits are being deducted from the compensation payment being ordered.

The impact of interim payments on final judgment calculations

At the conclusion of the substantive claim, should the Court have to make a judgment in respect of the quantification of damages to be awarded to the Injured Person, then the impact of an application for an interim payment, and its interaction with the CRB, resonates through to the terms of the final judgment. The interim payment/s awarded and the repayment of benefits to the Secretary of State will need to be detailed in the final judgment.

There are two Practice Directions in the CPR to consider at this juncture, ***CPR 25B PD.5*** and ***CPR 40B PD.5***, these provide for how final judgment figures are calculated in cases where interim payments have been made. ***CPR 25B PD.5*** states:

> *5.1 In this paragraph 'judgment' means:*
>
> *(1) any order to pay a sum of money,*
>
> *(2) a final award of damages,*
>
> *(3) an assessment of damages.*
>
> *5.2 In a final judgment where an interim payment has previously been made which is less than the total amount awarded by the judge, the order should set out in a preamble:*
>
> *(1) the total amount awarded by the judge, and*

(2) *the amounts and dates of the interim payment(s).*

5.3 *The total amount awarded by the judge should then be reduced by the total amount of any interim payments, and an order made for entry of judgment and payment of the balance.*

5.4 *In a final judgment where an interim payment has previously been made which is more than the total amount awarded by the judge, the order should set out in a preamble:*

(1) *the total amount awarded by the judge, and*

(2) *the amounts and dates of the interim payment(s).*

5.5 *An order should then be made for repayment, reimbursement, variation or discharge under rule 25.8(2) and for interest on an overpayment under rule 25.8(5).*

5.6 *Practice Direction 40B provides further information concerning adjustment of the final judgment sum.*

CPR 40B PD.5 states:

5.1 *In a final judgment where some or all of the damages awarded –*

(1) *fall under the heads of damage set out in column 1 of Schedule 2 to the Social Security (Recovery of Benefits) Act 1997 ('the 1997 Act') in respect of recoverable benefits received by the claimant set out in column 2 of that Schedule; and*

(2) *where the defendant has paid to the Secretary of State the recoverable benefits in accordance with the certificate (as defined in rule 36.15(1)(e)), there will be stated in the pre-*

amble to the judgment or order the amount awarded under each head of damage and the amount by which it has been reduced in accordance with section 8 of and Schedule 2 to the 1997 Act.

5.1A Where damages are awarded in a case where a lump sum payment (to be construed in accordance with section 1A of the 1997 Act) has been made to a dependant, then section 15 of the 1997 Act (as modified by Schedule 1 to the Social Security (Recovery of Benefits) (Lump Sum Payments) Regulations 2008 sets out what the court order must contain.

5.2 The judgment or order should then provide for entry of judgment and payment of the balance.

Therefore, when approaching the issue of adjusting the final payment figures at the conclusion of the substantive claim, the first issue to consider is whether the final order falls within the meaning of 'judgment' as set out in paragraph 5.1 of Practice Direction 25 in being a final award or assessment of damages. Should it do so then the order must set out the value of the interim payments made.

The Court must then apply the Practice Direction at CPR 40B PD.5. Should the Compensator have discharged any CRB's prior to the date of the judgment, and there have been any benefits, which are capable of being offset against the damages awarded, the order must contain the details as to the amount of each head of damage being awarded. The order must then provide for the amount of the reduction for the applicable benefit that is being offset. After the applicable reductions have been made, the Court order can provide for judgment of the balance of damages to be paid to the Injured Person.

NHS charges

NHS charges are considered in more detail in chapter eight of this book. It is worth noting at this stage that, if a Compensator makes an interim payment of damages then they not only have to discharge payment of the CRB, but they also have to discharge payment of the NHS charges certificate incurred up to the date of the interim payment of damages as well.

Pursuant to ***s150 of the Health and Social Care (Community Health Standards) Act (2003)***, liability to repay NHS charges arises upon the Compensator making a compensation payment. It is not contingent upon that compensation payment being a final payment in conclusion of the claim for damages.

CHAPTER SEVEN
MULTIPLE COMPENSATORS

A multiple compensator ('multi-comp') case is a case where there is more than one Compensator involved. From the outset of such a case, and for practical reasons, it is often helpful for the numerous Compensators to agree a lead co-ordinating Compensator to liaise with the CRU and the Injured Person on the issue of CRU liabilities. Often, but not always, this is the Compensator with the most significant liability.

It is not uncommon for a Compensator to take over conduct of the case from an insurance company or from other Compensators should they determine the issue of liability between themselves. Should this situation arise, and should the case have already been registered with the CRU, the Compensator taking over conduct of the case needs to notify the CRU of this development in the case so that the CRU can liaise with the correct Compensator. The Compensator with conduct should file form CRU 1 (Sol) with the CRU to notify them of the change of details.

The first important point to note in a multi-comp case is that the CRB belongs to the case, not the individual Compensator. Once a compensation payment is made, the Compensator making the payment of damages is liable to pay the Secretary of State an amount equal to the amount shown on the CRB. Each Compensator who makes a payment to the Injured Person is liable to repay the amount shown on the CRB at the date of their settlement, as will be recalled from previous chapters, ***s6(1) of the Recovery of Benefits Act*** states:

> *"A person who makes a compensation payment in any case is liable to pay to the Secretary of State an amount equal to the amount of the recoverable benefits".*

A Compensator therefore needs to ensure that they protect their position. It is clearly not in the best interests of a Compensator to be settling the claim at an earlier stage to the other Compensators and be exposed to paying the full value of the CRB, should any of the other Compensators be contributing to the settlement. Liaison between Compensators and the CRU in such cases is vital and if one Compensator takes over the claim from another Compensator then they must notify the CRU in writing of this.

In more straightforward multi-comp cases, the Compensators will reach a settlement with the Injured Person all at the same time on a global settlement basis. In such a case, the settlement date for all of the Compensators will be the same, and in such a case, the Compensators should work together, to apportion their individual liability in order to ensure the Secretary of State receives the total amount on the CRB.

In more complex cases, where one Compensator may wish to settle their liability in the claim earlier than the others, then that Compensator needs to consider their liability in respect of the CRB. The Compensator may need to acknowledge that they may repay the full level of the CRB and be reliant upon a Review and/or appeal being made in order to reduce their liability.

Example

The above text sets out the background to approaching a multi-comp case. When looking at the matter in practical terms, let us examine a two Compensator claim. The claim settles and the settlement date is the same for both Compensators. Compensator 1 pays compensation to the Injured Person before Compensator 2. The total amount of recoverable benefits due at the settlement is £50,000. The Compensators are liable to the Injured Person in the following percentage terms:

- Compensator 1 – 30% liable

- Compensator 2 – 70% liable

If the Compensators have engaged with each other and the CRU to agree an apportionment of their liabilities, then Compensator 1 will be liable to repay the CRU £15,000, and Compensator 2 will be liable to repay the CRU£35,000. The Compensators must bear in mind their liability under ***s6(1) of the Recovery of Benefits Act*** set out above. When a Compensator makes a compensation payment, they are liable for the total amount on the CRB regardless of their percentage liability to the Injured Person.

The financial services compensation scheme

A difficulty can arise if one Compensator is insolvent or their business has failed before the liability to the CRU is paid. In such circumstances, the solvent Compensator will wish to ensure that they are not left liable for the full value of the CRB when they are only liable for a portion of the injured party's damages. The first point to take note of is that the CRU are entitled to pursue the total amount on the CRB. As will be remembered from earlier chapters, the CRU have various enforcement powers at their disposal and can bring an action in the civil Court to recover any payments not made by the Compensators.

The Financial Services Compensation Scheme ('FSCS'), can assist in payment of the liabilities of an insolvent Compensator. The FSCS exists to protect customers of financial services firms that have failed. If the Compensator has failed and cannot pay claims against it, the FSCS can step in to pay compensation. Solvent Compensators should take note of the fact that any shortfall created by the involvement of the FSCS must be repaid by the solvent Compensators involved in the claim, which can of course lead to an increased financial liability on the solvent Compensator. This particular issue can be seen more in cases involving long tail disease issues where Compensators may no longer exist due to the historic nature of the claim.

Offsetting

When Compensators are making settlement offers to the Injured Person in multi-comp cases, the principles of offsetting are the same as with cases where there is only one Compensator. Any benefits being offset against the offer must be offset in accordance ***s8 of the Recovery of Benefits Act*** and ***Regulations 10 and 11 of the Social Security (Recovery of Benefits) (Lump Sum Payments) Regulations 2008***, the presence of additional Compensators does not alter this fundamental rule.

NHS charges

NHS charges are addressed in detail later on in this book, but it should be noted at this stage that, unlike the Recovery of Benefits Act, The Health and Social Care (Community Health and Standards) Act 2003, makes provision for the apportionment of liability to pay NHS charges where more than one Compensator is involved. This is contingent upon evidence being provided to enable the CRU to determine the liability, of each Compensator. This position is contrasted with the Recovery of Benefits Act, which does not permit apportionment of benefits payments between Compensators as discussed above.

The CRU's powers to apportion NHS charges stems from ***s153(5)(e) of the Health and Social Care (Community Health and Standards) Act 2003***, which provides:

> *for cases in which liability under section 150(2) is to be apportioned between two or more persons making compensation payments to or in respect of the same injured person in consequence of the same injury.*

CHAPTER EIGHT
NHS CHARGES

In previous chapters, we have looked at a Compensator's liability for applicable benefits that may be recovered by the Secretary of State. Separate to a Compensator's liability to repay applicable benefits to the CRU, is the Compensator's liability to repay any applicable NHS charges, if the Injured Person received NHS care as a result of the Compensator's negligent actions. Recovery of NHS charges is subject to two separate schemes. This chapter only examines the second scheme, as the first scheme addresses cases of road traffic accidents that occurred before 29 January 2007, and now has little relevance to the majority of current cases.

Imposition of liability

The Compensator's liability to repay NHS charges arises through ***Part 3 of The Health and Social Care (Community Health Standards) Act (2003)*** ('the Health and Social Care Act'). This provides that a person is liable to pay the NHS charges if they make a compensation payment in consequence of any injury suffered where the Injured Person has received NHS treatment at an NHS hospital, and/or been provided with NHS ambulance services. This legislation came into force on 29 January 2007. Prior to this, the Road Traffic (NHS Charges) Act (1999) also applied to NHS repayment charges, but this was repealed by ***s169 Health and Social Care Act***, and will not be considered further in this book.

The liability on the Compensator to repay NHS charges arises under ***s150 Health and Social Care Act***, which provides:

> *(1) This section applies if—*

(a) a person makes a compensation payment to or in respect of any other person (the "injured person") in consequence of any injury, whether physical or psychological, suffered by the injured person, and

(b) the injured person has—

(i) received NHS treatment at a health service hospital as a result of the injury,

(ii) been provided with NHS ambulance services as a result of the injury for the purpose of taking him to a health service hospital for NHS treatment (unless he was dead on arrival at that hospital), or

(iii) received treatment as mentioned in sub-paragraph (i) and been provided with ambulance services as mentioned in sub-paragraph (ii).

(2) The person making the compensation payment is liable to pay the relevant NHS charges—

(a) in respect of—

(i) the treatment, in so far as received at a hospital in England or Wales,

(ii) the ambulance services, in so far as provided to take the injured person to such a hospital, to the Secretary of State.

The Injured Person does not need to have sustained a physical injury for the liability under the Health and Social Care Act to arise, the injury can be psychological as well as physical. If the Injured Person therefore seeks damages for a recognised psychiatric disorder then the liability to repay the charges can arise.

Applying for a certificate of NHS charges

The NHS charges certificate is applied for at the same time as the CRB. As readers will recall from chapter three, the CRU registration information contains provision for the Compensator to provide information about the hospitals that the Injured Person attended as a result of the accident. This will enable the CRU to issue an NHS charges certificate. As with the application for the CRB, if inaccurate or insufficient information is provided then the NHS charges certificate can be amended if further information comes to light.

Similar to the position with a CRB, before a Compensator makes a compensation payment the NHS charges certificate ought to be obtained, ***s151(1) Health and Social Care Act*** provides:

> *Before a person makes a compensation payment in consequence of any injury suffered by an injured person, he may apply for a certificate to the Secretary of State, the Scottish Ministers or both, according to whether he believes the relevant NHS charges payable by him (if any) would be due to the Secretary of State, the Scottish Ministers or both.*

Readers will note the use of the word 'may' in this section of the Act, and how it compares to the provision of ***s4(1) Recovery of Benefits Act*** outlined earlier in this book, which imposes a mandatory requirement upon the Compensator to apply for a CRB before making a compensation payment. In practice if the Compensator notifies the CRU of the details of any hospital where the Injured Person received treatment, the NHS Charges Certificate will be issued by the CRU around the time of the CRB.

Again, in a similar manner to the CRB, the NHS charges certificate will remain in force for certain durations, ***s151(3) Health and Social Care Act*** provides:

> *(3) A certificate may provide that it is to remain in force—*

(a) until a specified date,

(b) until the occurrence of a specified event, or

(c) indefinitely.

As experienced practitioners will be aware, the CRU can and do issue NHS charges certificates after a claim has settled. Unlike a CRB, an NHS charges certificate can be issued post settlement, this is because the Compensator's liability is not extinguished by settlement of the claim and there is no provision in the Health and Social Care Act requiring the certificate to be issued within four weeks, as there is with the CRB.

Unlike benefits listed in a CRB, it is not possible to offset NHS charges against any heads of loss advanced in the substantive claim. Should an NHS charges certificate be issued after settlement of the claim, a Compensator is therefore not prejudiced by a late service of an NHS certificate, even if it arrives after the damages have been paid to the Injured Person.

Repayment of applicable NHS charges

To incur the liability for repayment of NHS charges, the Compensator has to make a payment of compensation, ***s150(3) Health and Social Care Act*** defines a compensation payment as:

(3) "Compensation payment" means a payment, including a payment in money's worth, made—

(1) by, or on behalf of, a person who is, or is alleged to be, liable to any extent in respect of the injury, or

(2) in pursuit of a compensation scheme for motor accident.

The definition of 'compensation payment' covers any payment made, even where liability is denied for example. Whether liability is admitted or not is irrelevant to whether the NHS charges are to be repaid, ***s150(14) Health and Social Care Act*** provides:

> *For the purposes of this Part, it is irrelevant whether a compensation payment is made with or without an admission of liability.*

The definition also includes payments made in money's worth, which would include, for example gift vouchers or providing physiotherapy to the Injured Person. These would constitute a compensation payment and a Compensator who provides a non-monetary 'gesture' to an Injured Person may therefore incur a liability to repay NHS charges. If a Compensator is making an ex gratia payment they therefore need to consider what additional liabilities in the form of NHS charges they are going to be required to pay as a result of the ex gratia payment.

The Compensator must pay the amount shown on the certificate of NHS Charges to the CRU within 14 days of either making a compensation payment, regardless of whether it is an interim payment or a payment in full and final settlement of the claim for damages; or the issuing of the certificate of NHS Charges, if that is after the date of the compensation payment.

Amount of NHS charges

The NHS charges certificate will set out the charges which will be repaid to the Secretary of State, ***s153(1)&(2) Health and Social Care Act*** provides:

> *(1) A certificate must specify the amount (or amounts) for which the person to whom it is issued is liable under section 150(2).*

(2) The amount (or amounts) to be specified is (or are) to be that (or those) set out in, or determined in accordance with, regulations, reduced if applicable in accordance with subsection (3) or regulations under subsection (10).

The amount of NHS charges is governed by a tariff. The current tariff scheme sets out the following charges:

Incident date (on or after)	**Out-patient**	**In-patient**	**Cap**	**Ambulance charges**
Pre 2.7.1997	£295	£435	£3,000	
02.07.1997	£354	£435	£10,000	
01.01.2003	£440	£541	£30,000	
01.04.2003	£452	£556	£33,000	
01.04.2004	£473	£582	£34,800	
01.04.2005	£483	£593	£35,500	
01.04.2006	£505	£620	£37,100	
29.01.2007	£505	£620	£37,100	£159
01.04.2008	£547	£672	£40,179	£165
01.04.2009*	£566	£695	£41,545	£171
01.04.2010	£585	£719	£42,999	£177
01.04.2011	£600	£737	£44,056	£181
01.04.2012	£615	£755	£45,153	£185
01.04.2013	£627	£770	£46,046	£189
01.04.2014	£637	£783	£46,831	£192
01.04.2015	£647	£796	£47,569	£195
01.04.2016	£665	£817	£48,849	£201
01.04.2017	£678	£833	£49,824	£205
01.04.2018	£688	£846	£50,561	£208
01.04.2019	£725	£891	£53,278	£219
01.04.2020	£743	£913	£54,566	£224

As can be seen, the tariff varies year by year and is calculated depending upon the extent of treatment that is given by the NHS. The amount of the charges that are repayable is subject to a cap, so in the most serious of cases, if the Injured Person requires extensive levels of treatment, the Compensator's liability is not open ended, but ceases when the cap figure is reached.

The period in respect of which NHS charges may be recovered by the DWP begins on the first day that treatment was provided following the incident, it ends on:

- the day a compensation payment is made in final discharge of a claim
- the date an agreement is made under which an earlier compensation payment is treated as having made in final discharge of any claim or
- when the appropriate tariff limit is reached

Example

The above text sets out the background law to the NHS charges scheme, now let us look at how the charges can be calculated in a claim.

If the Injured Person is taken to hospital in an ambulance on 2 April 2020, and remains an in-patient for five days the NHS charges certificate is calculated as follows:

Ambulance charges:	£224
In-patient charges:	£4,565 (5 days charges at £913 per day)
Total charges:	£4,789

Contributory negligence

Whilst it is not possible to offset any NHS charges against any heads of loss of damage, ***s153(3)(a) Health and Social Care Act*** provides that if any settlement or award is reduced for contributory negligence then the amount of NHS charges can be reduced in proportion to the contributory negligence reduction. This provides that:

> *If a certificate relates to a claim made by or on behalf of an injured person—*
>
> *(a) in respect of which a court in England and Wales or Scotland has ordered a reduction of damages in accordance with section 1 of the Law Reform (Contributory Negligence) Act 1945 (c. 28),*
>
> ...
>
> *the amount (or amounts) specified in the certificate is (or are) to be that (or those) which would be so specified apart from this subsection, reduced by the same proportion as the reduction of damages.*

Compensators should note that if any reduction for contributory negligence is made to the NHS charges, then evidence of the written agreement made between the litigants as to the percentage reduction, must be filed with the CRU to support the reduction of the NHS charges.

The CRU's Technical Guidance Note states that a signed report detailing the terms of the agreement and, that those terms were agreed in a fair and open manner should be filed with the CRU. In practise, this does not always happen and offer and acceptance letters detailing the agreement for the contributory negligence reduction can be filed, these are often accepted by the CRU as evidence of the agreed reduction. Telephone notes do not constitute a signed report and should not be relied upon, an attempt by a Compensator to do so may result in the evidence being rejected, and the Compensator being financially prejudiced. Ultimately, the Compensator will wish to put before the CRU clear written evidence that there has been an agreed reduction for contributory negligence from the compensation award.

Where the reduction for contributory negligence is made by the court, the evidence is easy to collate for the CRU to consider, a copy of the court order can be provided. In cases where the parties to the substantive litigation reach an agreed reduction for contributory negligence, the Compensator has to be more careful as to the evidential trail that is kept to provide to the CRU.

Example

Let us look at the previous example again. The Injured Person was taken to hospital in an ambulance on 2 April 2020 and remained an in-patient for five days, the certificate was therefore calculated as follows:

Ambulance charges:	£224
In-patient charges:	£4,565 (5 days charges at £913 per day)
Total charges:	£4,789

If there had been an agreed reduction in contributory negligence of 15%, then the liability of the Compensator to the CRU for the NHS charges would now be £4,070.65.

Multiple compensators

If there is more than one Compensator involved in the claim and who will be liable for repayment of NHS charges, then the NHS charges can be apportioned between those Compensators. As with the CRB, Compensators should liaise between themselves and the CRU to ensure that they are clear as to how their liabilities will be apportioned. In such cases, the Compensators should contact the CRU as soon as possible to confirm if an apportionment is being carried out, and if so whether a particular Compensator is taking the lead in co-ordinating with the CRU, or whether the Compensators are not co-ordinating the settlement of NHS charges.

The details of the agreed apportionment need to be provided to the CRU who can then assess what sums will be repaid by the particular Compensators. The CRU will then advise the Compensators on the evidence of the agreement over the liability that they have to the CRU, and a revised NHS certificate can then be issued to the Compensators.

The Health and Social Care Act makes provision for apportionment of liability to pay NHS charges where more than one Compensator is involved, this position was discussed in the chapter addressing multi-comp cases. As readers will recall, the CRU can apportion the amount of relevant NHS charges that would be payable by each Compensator, if evidence is provided to enable the CRU to determine the liability, of each Compensator.

Fatal accidents

Since 29 January 2007, NHS charges have not been recoverable for fatal accidents where the compensation payment has been paid solely in accordance with the Fatal Accidents Act (1976), ('the 1976 Act'). However, if compensation (or an element of it) was paid under the Law Reform (Miscellaneous Provisions) Act (1934), ('the 1934 Act'), there will be a liability on the Compensator to pay NHS charges.

It is important to distinguish between the damages awarded or agreed under each piece of legislation, as the purpose of each one is very different. The 1976 Act gives an independent right of action to relatives or 'dependants' of the deceased. This will allow relatives and dependents to recover damages such as bereavement damages, and loss of dependency or loss of income, caused by the death of the injured party. The 1934 Act allows claims to be made on behalf of the deceased's estate. These may have been made for:

- pain, suffering and loss suffered by the deceased
- loss of earnings and cost of care prior to their death

A claim made under the 1976 Act therefore does not attract a liability to repay NHS charges, as it is not brought in relation to the injuries suffered by the Injured Person. The Compensator will need to demonstrate that any payment was made solely under the 1976 Act, in order to evidence to the CRU that the NHS charges are not recoverable. In default of such evidence, NHS charges will be recoverable where no evidence can be provided of the Act under which the compensation payment was made.

A claim brought under the 1934 Act can attract a liability for NHS charges. As practitioners will be aware, sometimes the Injured Person does not die immediately following the accident, and can be aware of their medical condition for sometime prior to death, such a condition can sound in general damages.

The current Judicial College Guidelines, 15th edition, reflects the position that awards for such damages are judged by the knowledge of the injured party to their approaching death, any loss of amenity and the period of suffering. Furthermore, pursuant to ***Kadir v Mistry & Ors [2014] EWCA Civ 1177***, awards may also be made for 'mental anguish' caused by the fear of the curtailment of life. The current Judicial College Guidelines provide that damages can range up to an award of £22,350 for injuries resulting in death.

Therefore, if the Injured Person survived the accident, even for a short time, and required NHS care, then there may be a liability on the Compensator to repay those NHS charges.

As practitioners will see from the above, the CRU will not be aware of which Act the claim is being made under, and ultimately whether a compensation payment is being made under the 1934 or 1976 Act. The CRU will always issue a certificate of NHS charges in fatal accident cases. The duty is on the Compensator/s to notify the CRU of the provisions of the claim and settlement and to ultimately challenge the NHS charges certificate if the charges do not apply. The documentation that demonstrates that the compensation payment was made solely under the 1976 Act will need to be filed with the CRU, as the CRU will not be able to review the NHS charges certificate without such documentation.

Regardless of the legislation under which the compensation payment falls, no NHS charges are payable where the Injured Person has been declared dead on arrival at the hospital. Therefore, from a practical perspective, an analysis of any hospital records is required to assess the time and location of declared death.

CHAPTER NINE
THE CRU REVIEW AND APPEALS PROCESS

The Review and Appeals process allows the Compensator or Injured Person the opportunity to seek a reconsideration of the CRB and/or NHS charges certificate. This is the final limb of the CRU process and can be the area where a party can reduce or recover monies owed or paid to the Secretary of State.

There are three paths open to a party who wishes to challenge the content of a CRB or NHS certificate. They are; firstly a Review; secondly a Request for a Mandatory Reconsideration; and thirdly an Appeal. Each of these paths will be discussed in this chapter.

The fundamental premise of seeking a Review of or commencing an Appeal of a CRB is that receipt of a benefit by the Injured Person is not enough of itself to bring the Recovery of Benefits Act into operation and require repayment by the Compensator. It must be shown that there is a sufficient link between the injury or disease and the payment of the benefit, failing which a Compensator has no liability for the benefit received by the Injured Person. As set out in ***s1(1) Recovery of Benefits Act***:

> *(1) This Act applies in cases where—*
>
> *(a) a person makes a payment (whether on his own behalf or not) to or in respect of any other person in consequence of any accident, injury or disease suffered by the other, and*
>
> *(b) any listed benefits have been, or are likely to be, paid to or for the other during the relevant period in respect of the accident, injury or disease.*

There is an extensive amount of case law arising from the First Tier Tribunal of the Social Entitlement Chamber (where CRU appeals are heard) on what constitutes a benefit paid *'in respect of the accident, injury or disease'*. By their very nature, the questions about whether there is a sufficient link between the injury or disease and the payment of the benefit/s will turn on the facts and the medical evidence of each case.

It is not intended to analyse each decision of the First Tier and Upper Tribunals in this text. Firstly the judgments of the First Tier Tribunal of the Social Entitlement Chamber are not binding, and are therefore of limited persuasive value when relied upon in an appeal. Secondly, given their fact specific nature they would be extremely voluminous and time consuming for readers to consider in order to review the principles of challenging a CRB. The principles are neatly encapsulated in Chapter 5 of ***Kemp & Kemp Commentary, 5-079***, which sets out the following:

> *The mere fact that a claimant was receiving benefit before the accident, that there is a change in the basis on which a claimant is receiving benefit before and after an accident, or that a claimant would have received a different benefit even had the accident not occurred, does not render benefit irrecoverable. In some cases, however, the claimant may be entitled to claim damages representing the benefits lost.*
>
> — *Contributory negligence, or non-related contributory causes, do not affect the recoverability of the whole amount of benefit.*
>
> — *The whole of a payment of benefit is recoverable, including elements received for members of a claimant's family.*
>
> — *Generally, the accident need not be the sole cause of a payment of benefit but must be an effective cause.*

— *In particular, separate causes of the payment of benefit (whether pre-dating or post-dating the relevant accident, and whether arising naturally or as a result of an accident) must give rise to the payment of benefit irrespective of the effects of the accident if the benefit is to be irrecoverable.*

— *If neither the accident nor the other factors would have caused the payment of benefit of themselves but cause the benefit to be paid in combination, the benefit is recoverable. This will be particularly relevant to claims relating to psychiatric injury. If a claimant's symptoms "wax and wane", then provided the matters in respect of which complaint is made remain an effective cause of the symptoms, benefit will be recoverable.*

— *Benefits are paid "in respect of" an accident if they are paid as a result of the symptoms resulting from an operation undergone by the claimant in response to the relevant incident or where psychological injury results from a misdiagnosis.] However, a negligent act might break the causal link between the accident and the payment of benefit.*

— *If benefits should never have been paid at all, then a compensator may appeal on the basis that they were not paid "in respect of" the accident.*

— *If the claimant received benefit at a higher rate than he or she should have done, an appeal can be made against recovery of the excess.*

— *The burden of proof that benefit would not have been paid in the absence of the relevant injury or disease, or should not have been paid, rests on the person challenging the decision] The CRU must first, however, produce "evidence showing a prima facie connection between the injury and the payment of benefit, so as to explain the listing of the benefit on the certificate of recoverable benefits in the first place".*

Parties seeking to challenge the CRB should note the decision in the case of ***Hassall v Secretary of State for Social Security; Pether v Secretary of State for Social Security [1995] 3 All ER 909***. This provides that when assessing whether or not the benefit has been paid to the Injured Person, the person conducting the Review, Mandatory Reconsideration or Appeal, was not limited to considering whether the part of the benefit was solely paid in respect of the Injured Person's support. It also included those parts that were calculated for the support of his wife and children. As such the decision to award the benefits may take into consideration circumstances wider than the Injured Person's condition.

Preliminary

Should a Compensator seek to challenge a CRB then, as discussed in chapter four, they are best advised to consider this issue when they are making their settlement offer. This is because the terms of the settlement offer need to be considered by the CRU and can affect the recovery of any monies in this process. When drafting the offer, the Offeror will have needed to have identified whether any offsets are being made. The next point the Offeror should have considered when making the settlement offer is whether they wish to retain any monies recovered through the Review/Appeal process or whether they wish the monies to be repaid to the other party.

If the Compensator is seeking to appeal the CRB, and the Compensator wishes to retain any monies recovered in the appeals process, then the Compensator should consider whether they have an agreement with the Injured Person that the monies will be retained by the Compensator. In the first instance, the Compensator needs to consider if they have reduced the compensation payment by any applicable benefits, if so by how much. As will be recalled from chapter four addressing settlement offers, the Compensator may make a settlement offer without reduction of the CRB.

If the Compensator reduces the compensation and the CRB is later reduced through a Reconsideration and/or Appeal, then the Compensator is obliged to recalculate the compensation award. Pursuant to ***Hilton International Hotels v Smith [1002] PIQR P14***, the monies are then to be refunded to the Injured Person. In such circumstances, and in the absence of an agreement to the contrary, the Compensator will have incurred the costs of reviewing/appealing the CRB, only to receive no return for its efforts.

When making a Part 36 Offer it is advisable to insert a clause into the offer providing that any monies recovered in a Mandatory Reconsideration or Appeal will be retained by the Compensator. If the substantive claim is settled by way of a Calderbank Offer embodied in a Court Order, then the Compensator should ensure that there is a paragraph in the Order providing such a term. The aim for the Compensator needs to be, to ensure that there is evidence to exhibit to the Mandatory Reconsideration and/or Appeal documents that are lodged with the CRU showing that the parties agree that the Compensator retains the benefit of any monies recovered, otherwise the Compensator's work may all be for nought.

Review

The first path open to parties who wish to challenge a CRB is to ask for a Review of the CRB. Pursuant to ***s10 Recovery of Benefits Act:***

> *(1) Any certificate of recoverable benefits may be reviewed by the Secretary of State—*
>
> *(a) either within the prescribed period or in prescribed cases or circumstances; and*

(b) either on an application made for the purpose or on his own initiative.

(2) On a review under this section the Secretary of State may either —

(a) confirm the certificate, or

(b) (subject to subsection (3)) issue a fresh certificate containing such variations as he considers appropriate or.

(c) revoke the certificate.

(3) The Secretary of State may not vary the certificate so as to increase the total amount of the recoverable benefits unless it appears to him that the variation is required as a result of the person who applied for the certificate supplying him with incorrect or insufficient information.

A Review can be commenced very simply, it is initiated by the aggrieved party sending its written position to the CRU and asking for the CRB to be reviewed. Parties can write to the CRU at any time during the case and ask the CRU to formally Review the CRB and amend any head of benefit listed therein. A Review request must be made in writing and the party must give their reasons as to why it is thought the CRB is wrong. Any evidence that is thought to be helpful should also be included with the Review request.

The CRU Technical Guidance Note sets out that a Review may be made on the following grounds:

- *the CRB was issued in ignorance of, or based on a mistake as to, a material fact;*
- *a mistake was made in the preparation of the CRB;*

- *incorrect or insufficient information was supplied to the Secretary of State by the person who applied for the CRB and, as a result, the amount of benefit or lump sum payment specified in the CRB was less than it would have been had the information supplied been correct or sufficient;*
- *a ground for appeal is satisfied under Section 11 of the 1997 Act.*

The grounds under ***s11 Recovery of Benefits Act*** are:

(a) that any amount, rate or period specified in the certificate is incorrect, or

(b) that listed benefits which have been, or are likely to be, paid otherwise than in respect of the accident, injury or disease in question have been brought into account or.

(c) that listed benefits which have not been, and are not likely to be, paid to the injured person during the relevant period have been brought into account, or

(d) that the payment on the basis of which the certificate was issued is not a payment within section 1(1)(a) of the 1997 Act.

When a CRB is reviewed, the CRU will consider a range of factors, these include; the types of benefits and lump sum payments listed on the CRB as being recoverable; the amounts paid to the Injured Person and the periods over which those payments have been or are likely to be paid. Any errors, omissions or other changes, which may affect the outcome of the review, will be taken into account, even if they are unrelated to the reasons for requesting the review. The CRU's powers to consider all of the facts of the case are clear, and the Review can consider a wide variety of factors in order to reach the correct decision about the applicability of the benefits.

When conducting a Review, the CRU has a variety of powers that it can exercise. These are:

- there may be no amendment to the CRB and the CRU may confirm in writing that the CRB is correct
- revoke the CRB and issue a fresh one
- change the CRB and issue a fresh one

If the Review is successful and a revised CRB is issued, it will cover the same period as the CRB it replaces. As set out above, one of the grounds on which a CRU Review may be made is that incorrect or insufficient information was supplied to the Secretary of State by the person who applied for the CRB.

Following a Review, it is possible for the CRU to issue a fresh CRB showing an increase in the amount of recoverable benefits, if the Compensator failed to provide to the CRU correct or sufficient information. Should such a circumstance arise, then the Compensator will be liable to pay the difference between the two CRB's to CRU. As readers will recall from chapter three, if incorrect or insufficient information is provided to the CRU, then the CRU has a right to issue a revised CRB.

Mandatory Reconsideration

At the conclusion of the substantive claim, and when the monies set out in the CRB have been repaid, the parties may apply for a Mandatory Reconsideration of the CRB. Prior to the implementation of the Welfare Reform Act, the process by which a CRB was appealed was very different. The Welfare Reform Act introduced changes from 28 October 2013 to the appeals process. The new process provides that more disputes against DWP decisions can be resolved without the need for referral to the First Tier Tribunal of the Social Entitlement

Chamber. ***s102 Welfare Reform Act*** amended ***s12 Social Security Act (1998)***, and required that before an appeal can be brought the Secretary of State has to have considered whether to revise the original decision.

The Mandatory Reconsideration provision that is now in place provides for a consideration on the papers of the evidence in a case, and allows the DWP to make a decision about any revisions to the CRB without the need for an oral hearing.

When making the request for a Mandatory Reconsideration, the CRU is being given the opportunity to formally reconsider its decision without the need for an appeal being made. The applicant party needs to outline their reasons, in writing, for requesting the Mandatory Reconsideration. The party seeking the Mandatory Reconsideration can seek the Reconsideration on one or more of the following grounds:

1. Any amount, rate or period of benefit specified on the CRB is wrong

2. The CRB shows benefits and/or lump sum payments which were not paid as a result of the accident, injury or disease

3. Benefits and/or lump sum payments listed on the CRB which have not and are not likely to be paid to the Injured Person have been taken into account

4. The compensation payment made was not as a consequence of the accident, injury or disease

It is not uncommon in practise for the appellant to rely upon multiple grounds when seeking a Mandatory Reconsideration and/or Appeal. When commencing a Mandatory Reconsideration the party applying for the Reconsideration must file various documents that were obtained in the substantive claim, these include: all medical reports and any surveillance evidence obtained by both parties; copies of any statements;

copies of the Particulars of Claim; copies of the documents from both parties which confirm the details of the settlement. In addition, any document that a party considers supports its argument for a Mandatory Reconsideration should also be filed. This means that Mandatory Reconsiderations are often a 'document heavy' process, but in the absence of assessing all of the medical evidence the CRU is denied the opportunity to review the complete medical picture and assess whether any part of the CRB should be refunded.

The Grounds for the Mandatory Reconsideration should then be lodged with the CRU for their consideration. The CRU will then look at all of the evidence and decide if the CRB should be:

- changed and a partial refund issued
- revoked and a full refund issued
- confirmed as correct

When a decision is reached, the CRU will issue an explanation of the decision in writing, much akin to a judgment. This decision is known as a Mandatory Reconsideration Notice, and a party will need to obtain this should they wish to proceed to appeal the Reconsideration decision.

There are time scales to consider in seeking to submit an application for a Mandatory Reconsideration or Appeal, and a Mandatory Reconsideration must be made within one month of paying the CRU the money due as listed on the CRB.

Appeal

Should the application for a Mandatory Reconsideration not be successful, or be successful only in part, then the next course of action open to a party is to appeal the Mandatory Reconsideration Notice. An appeal cannot be made until the substantive compensation claim is settled and all monies due as listed on the CRB have been paid in full to the CRU. The appeal is made to the First Tier Tribunal of the Social Entitlement Chamber. An appeal may be made by the Compensator and/or the Injured Person.

As with the Mandatory Reconsideration, there are strict time limits within which an appeal must be brought. Any appeal must be made within one month of the date the Mandatory Reconsideration Notice being sent. Should the time limits for an Appeal be breached then the Tribunal Services will require an explanation for the delay. The Tribunal Judge will need to analyse the reasons provided for not appealing in time and then decide if the appeal can be accepted. The Tribunal Judge will look at:

- whether there were special circumstances for the delay
- the length of time since the compensator paid the money to the CRU
- whether it is in the interests of natural justice that the appeal is accepted
- whether the appeal is reasonably likely to succeed

Whilst not directly analogous it is likely that the test akin to that of relief from sanctions under ***CPR 3.9*** and the test set out in ***Denton v TH White Ltd [2014] EWCA Civ 906***, will be applied when considering the position. The defaulting party will therefore need to identify whether:

1. The breach of the time limit is serious and significant
2. The reason for the time limit being breached

3. In all the circumstances of the case should the appeal be allowed to proceed

When considering if an appeal should be commenced, the parties need to understand the decisions of the CRU at the Mandatory Reconsideration stage, for this reason, the Mandatory Reconsideration Notice obtained at the Mandatory Reconsideration stage is vital. The Notice is akin to the judgment of a lower Court which the appellate tribunal needs to consider when reaching its decision.

The appeal must be made in writing on the CRU's prescribed form, SSCS3, and sent directly to HMCTS. A copy of the Mandatory Reconsideration Notice must be filed and the appeal will not go ahead unless the Appellant includes a copy of this notification with the appeal. It is advisable to use the Tribunal's Notice of Appeal form to make the appeal.

The grounds for an appeal are set out in ***s11 Recovery of Benefits Act***, and state that an appeal against a CRB must be made on one or more of the following grounds:

(a) Any amount, rate or period specified in the CRB is wrong

(b) The CRB shows benefits and/or lump sum payments which were not paid as a result of the accident, injury or disease

(c) Benefits and/or lump sum payments listed which have not and are not likely to be paid to the injured person have been brought into account

(d) The compensation payment made was not made as a consequence of the accident, injury or disease

Appeals can be conducted on the papers or alternatively a party may request an oral hearing. If an oral hearing is requested then the case is heard before a Tribunal led by a Tribunal Judge assisted by a qualified member who is not from the DWP, the qualified member is medically qualified and provides assistance to the Tribunal Judge on the medical issues in the case. The tribunal can look at the evidence, law, and/or circumstances at the time the CRU made the decision which is being appealed. Therefore, the appellate Tribunal has a wide scope to consider the issues in the case before reaching its decision.

Much like a Mandatory Reconsideration, when considering the appeal, the Tribunal has various powers and may:

- change the CRB and issue a partial refund of any CRU monies
- revoke the CRB and issue a full refund of any CRU monies
- confirm that the decision of the Mandatory Reconsideration is correct

If the appeal is unsuccessful, the Appellant may ask the Tribunal for a Statement of Reasons as to its decision. Again, this is essentially the judgment of the Tribunal and gives a full explanation of the Tribunal's decision including the facts and relevant law used to make the decision. The Appellant can then analyse this decision and consider whether it wishes to avail itself of its further recourse, which is an appeal to the Upper Tier Tribunal. Before an Appellant can appeal to the Upper Tier Tribunal, the Appellant must have received a full Statement of Reasons of the First Tier Tribunal's decision and applied to the Tribunal Judge for permission to appeal.

Appeals to the Upper Tier Tribunal are rare and can only be made on a point of law. A party cannot appeal to the Upper Tier Tribunal about questions of fact or the First Tier Tribunal's medical findings or conclusions. Appeals to the Upper Tier Tribunal do not arise frequently and the Appellant must file the application for permission to appeal to an Upper Tribunal Judge. Again, an appeal to the Upper Tier Tribunal must be made within one month of the decision of the First Tier Tribunal.

NHS certificates

The process for seeking a Review and appealing the NHS certificate is not the same as for a CRB. The power to review an NHS charges certificate is contained at ***s156 Health and Social Care Act.*** If a party wishes to challenge the NHS certificate then the first step is still to seek a Review of the NHS certificate in the same manner as a party would when seeking to Review the CRB. The main difference in challenging NHS certificates and challenging CRB's, is that when challenging an NHS certificate there is no provision for a Mandatory Reconsideration. If the Review is not successful or only partially successful, then the recourse is to proceed to an appeal.

When an NHS charges certificate is reviewed ***s156(5) Health and Social Care Act*** gives the Secretary of State broadly the same powers as when a CRB is reviewed. The ***Health and Social Care Act*** gives the Secretary of State the following powers in relation to conducting a Review of an NHS charges certificate:

> *(5) On a review under or by virtue of this section, the Secretary of State or the Scottish Ministers may—*
>
> *(a) confirm the certificate,*
>
> *(b) issue a fresh certificate containing such variations as he considers or they consider appropriate, or*
>
> *(c) revoke the certificate.*

As with lodging an appeal against a CRB, there are time limits within which an appeal must be brought. A party seeking to appeal the NHS certificate must make the appeal no later than three calendar months after the latest of:

- the date on the Certificate of NHS charges or
- the date on which the compensation payment was made to the injured person or
- if the Certificate has been reviewed, the date the Certificate was confirmed or a fresh Certificate was issued

In a similar manner to the situation set out above concerning late appeals against CRB's, if the appeal is late, HMCTS will require an explanation for the delay. An appeal must be made on one or more of the following grounds:

- an amount specified in the Certificate of NHS charges is incorrect
- an amount specified takes into account treatment which is not NHS treatment received by the injured person, in respect of their injury, at an NHS hospital
- the ambulance which transported or treated the injured person, is not an NHS ambulance service
- the payment on the basis of which the Certificate of NHS charges was issued is not a compensation payment

Documents

As can be seen from the above, when a party is applying for a Review, Mandatory Reconsideration and/or Appeal of a certificate be it a CRB or NHS charges certificate, the CRU's decision is somewhat dependent upon what evidence it receives from the applicant. As set out above, the

CRU is entitled to see the documentation obtained by the parties in the substantive personal injury claim, and parties should take care to comply with the provisions regarding filing the necessary documentation.

The parties to the litigation need to bear in mind that pursuant to ***s110 Social Security Administration Act (1992)***, the DWP has the right to examine the records of Compensators to confirm that they are complying fully with the provisions of the Recovery of Benefits Act.

MORE BOOKS BY LAW BRIEF PUBLISHING

A selection of our other titles available now:-

'A Practical Guide to the General Data Protection Regulation (GDPR) – 2nd Edition' by Keith Markham
'Ellis on Credit Hire – Sixth Edition' by Aidan Ellis & Tim Kevan
'A Practical Guide to Working with Litigants in Person and McKenzie Friends in Family Cases' by Stuart Barlow
'Protecting Unregistered Brands: A Practical Guide to the Law of Passing Off' by Lorna Brazell
'A Practical Guide to Secondary Liability and Joint Enterprise Post-Jogee' by Joanne Cecil & James Mehigan
'A Practical Guide to the Pre-Action RTA Claims Protocol for Personal Injury Lawyers' by Antonia Ford
'A Practical Guide to Neighbour Disputes and the Law' by Alexander Walsh
'A Practical Guide to Forfeiture of Leases' by Mark Shelton
'A Practical Guide to Coercive Control for Legal Practitioners and Victims' by Rachel Horman
'A Practical Guide to Rights Over Airspace and Subsoil' by Daniel Gatty
'Tackling Disclosure in the Criminal Courts – A Practitioner's Guide' by Narita Bahra QC & Don Ramble
'A Practical Guide to the Law of Driverless Cars – Second Edition' by Alex Glassbrook, Emma Northey & Scarlett Milligan
'A Practical Guide to TOLATA Claims' by Greg Williams
'Artificial Intelligence – The Practical Legal Issues' by John Buyers
'A Practical Guide to the Law of Prescription in Scotland' by Andrew Foyle
'A Practical Guide to the Construction and Rectification of Wills and Trust Instruments' by Edward Hewitt
'A Practical Guide to the Law of Bullying and Harassment in the Workplace' by Philip Hyland

'How to Be a Freelance Solicitor: A Practical Guide to the SRA-Regulated Freelance Solicitor Model' by Paul Bennett
'A Practical Guide to Prison Injury Claims' by Malcolm Johnson
'A Practical Guide to the Small Claims Track' by Dominic Bright
'A Practical Guide to Advising Clients at the Police Station' by Colin Stephen McKeown-Beaumont
'A Practical Guide to Antisocial Behaviour Injunctions' by Iain Wightwick
'Practical Mediation: A Guide for Mediators, Advocates, Advisers, Lawyers, and Students in Civil, Commercial, Business, Property, Workplace, and Employment Cases' by Jonathan Dingle with John Sephton
'The Mini-Pupillage Workbook' by David Boyle
'A Practical Guide to Crofting Law' by Brian Inkster
'A Practical Guide to Spousal Maintenance' by Liz Cowell
'A Practical Guide to the Law of Domain Names and Cybersquatting' by Andrew Clemson
'A Practical Guide to the Law of Gender Pay Gap Reporting' by Harini Iyengar
'A Practical Guide to the Rights of Grandparents in Children Proceedings' by Stuart Barlow
'NHS Whistleblowing and the Law' by Joseph England
'Employment Law and the Gig Economy' by Nigel Mackay & Annie Powell
'A Practical Guide to Noise Induced Hearing Loss (NIHL) Claims' by Andrew Mckie, Ian Skeate, Gareth McAloon
'An Introduction to Beauty Negligence Claims – A Practical Guide for the Personal Injury Practitioner' by Greg Almond
'Intercompany Agreements for Transfer Pricing Compliance' by Paul Sutton
'Zen and the Art of Mediation' by Martin Plowman
'A Practical Guide to the SRA Principles, Individual and Law Firm Codes of Conduct 2019 – What Every Law Firm Needs to Know' by Paul Bennett
'A Practical Guide to Adoption for Family Lawyers' by Graham Pegg
'A Practical Guide to Industrial Disease Claims' by Andrew Mckie & Ian Skeate
'A Practical Guide to Redundancy' by Philip Hyland
'A Practical Guide to Vicarious Liability' by Mariel Irvine

‘A Practical Guide to Applications for Landlord’s Consent and Variation of Leases’ by Mark Shelton

‘A Practical Guide to Relief from Sanctions Post-Mitchell and Denton’ by Peter Causton

‘A Practical Guide to Equity Release for Advisors’ by Paul Sams

‘A Practical Guide to Unlawful Eviction and Harassment’ by Stephanie Lovegrove

‘A Practical Guide to the Law Relating to Food’ by Ian Thomas

‘A Practical Guide to Financial Services Claims’ by Chris Hegarty

‘The Law of Houses in Multiple Occupation: A Practical Guide to HMO Proceedings’ by Julian Hunt

‘A Practical Guide to Unlawful Eviction and Harassment’ by Stephanie Lovegrove

‘A Practical Guide to Solicitor and Client Costs’ by Robin Dunne

‘Occupiers, Highways and Defective Premises Claims: A Practical Guide Post-Jackson – 2nd Edition’ by Andrew Mckie

‘A Practical Guide to Financial Ombudsman Service Claims’ by Adam Temple & Robert Scrivenor

‘A Practical Guide to the Law of Enfranchisement and Lease Extension’ by Paul Sams

‘A Practical Guide to Marketing for Lawyers – 2nd Edition’ by Catherine Bailey & Jennet Ingram

'A Practical Guide to Advising Schools on Employment Law' by Jonathan Holden

‘A Practical Guide to Running Housing Disrepair and Cavity Wall Claims: 2nd Edition’ by Andrew Mckie & Ian Skeate

‘A Practical Guide to Holiday Sickness Claims – 2nd Edition’ by Andrew Mckie & Ian Skeate

‘Arguments and Tactics for Personal Injury and Clinical Negligence Claims’ by Dorian Williams

‘A Practical Guide to QOCS and Fundamental Dishonesty’ by James Bentley

‘A Practical Guide to Drone Law’ by Rufus Ballaster, Andrew Firman, Eleanor Clot

‘A Practical Guide to Compliance for Personal Injury Firms Working With Claims Management Companies’ by Paul Bennett

‘A Practical Guide to the Landlord and Tenant Act 1954: Commercial Tenancies’ by Richard Hayes & David Sawtell

'A Practical Guide to Dog Law for Owners and Others' by Andrea Pitt
'RTA Allegations of Fraud in a Post-Jackson Era: The Handbook – 2nd Edition' by Andrew Mckie
'RTA Personal Injury Claims: A Practical Guide Post-Jackson' by Andrew Mckie
'On Experts: CPR35 for Lawyers and Experts' by David Boyle
'An Introduction to Personal Injury Law' by David Boyle
'A Practical Guide to Claims Arising From Accidents Abroad and Travel Claims' by Andrew Mckie & Ian Skeate
'A Practical Guide to Chronic Pain Claims' by Pankaj Madan
'A Practical Guide to Claims Arising from Fatal Accidents' by James Patience
'A Practical Approach to Clinical Negligence Post-Jackson' by Geoffrey Simpson-Scott
'Employers' Liability Claims: A Practical Guide Post-Jackson' by Andrew Mckie
'A Practical Guide to Subtle Brain Injury Claims' by Pankaj Madan
'A Practical Guide to Costs in Personal Injury Cases' by Matthew Hoe
'The No Nonsense Solicitors' Practice: A Guide To Running Your Firm' by Bettina Brueggemann
'The Queen's Counsel Lawyer's Omnibus: 20 Years of Cartoons from The Times 1993-2013' by Alex Steuart Williams

These books and more are available to order online direct from the publisher at www.lawbriefpublishing.com, where you can also read free sample chapters. For any queries, contact us on 0844 587 2383 or mail@lawbriefpublishing.com.

Our books are also usually in stock at www.amazon.co.uk with free next day delivery for Prime members, and at good legal bookshops such as Wildy & Sons.

We are regularly launching new books in our series of practical day-to-day practitioners' guides. Visit our website and join our free newsletter to be kept informed and to receive special offers, free chapters, etc.

You can also follow us on Twitter at www.twitter.com/lawbriefpub.

www.ingramcontent.com/pod-product-compliance
Lightning Source LLC
LaVergne TN
LVHW022101200926
848481LV00003B/1028
9781912687824